Cafe Indiana Cookbook

Terrace Books, a trade imprint of the University of Wisconsin Press, takes its name from the Memorial Union Terrace, located at the University of Wisconsin–Madison. Since its inception in 1907, the Wisconsin Union has provided a venue for students, faculty, staff, and alumni to debate art, music, politics, and the issues of the day. It is a place where theater, music, drama, literature, dance, outdoor activities, and major speakers are made available to the campus and the community. To learn more about the Union, visit www.union.wisc.edu.

Cafe
INDIANA
~ ~ ~
# Cookbook

Joanne Raetz Stuttgen and Jolene Ketzenberger

TERRACE BOOKS

A trade imprint of the UNIVERSITY OF WISCONSIN PRESS

TERRACE BOOKS

A trade imprint of the University of Wisconsin Press
1930 Monroe Street, 3rd Floor
Madison, Wisconsin 53711-2059
uwpress.wisc.edu

3 Henrietta Street
London WC2E 8LU, England
eurospanbookstore.com

5   4   3   2   1

Printed in the United States of America

Library of Congress Cataloging-in-Publication Data

Stuttgen, Joanne Raetz, 1961–
Cafe Indiana cookbook / Joanne Raetz Stuttgen and Jolene Ketzenberger.
p. cm.
Includes bibliographical references and index.
ISBN 978-0-299-24994-6 (pbk. : alk. paper)
ISBN 978-0-299-24993-9 (e-book)
1. Cookery, American—Midwestern style. 2. Cookery—Indiana. 3. Restaurants—Indiana.
I. Ketzenberger, Jolene Phelps. II. Title.
TX715.2.M53S775   2010
641.5977—dc22   2010013126

Some of the sidebars are reproduced in slightly modified form from *Cafe Wisconsin Cookbook* (coauthored with Terese Allen) and *Cafe Indiana* and are used here with permission of the University of Wisconsin Press.

Contents

Preface

Get ready for some great eats.

The recipes in this cookbook are for favorite dishes at small-town cafes featured in Joanne's 2007 book, *Cafe Indiana*. Over a period of two years, Joanne visited more than 450 Main Street restaurants, eating more country-fried steak, salmon patties, and rhubarb pie than she had in her entire lifetime. With every bite, this Minnesota-born folklorist who has lived nearly twenty years in the land of the Indianapolis 500 and Hoosier Hysteria discovered that you really don't know folks at all until you know what it is they like to eat. Stop in at any small-town cafe across the state and you'll not only find a great meal, but you'll also get acquainted with some great people—and, if you're lucky, get a slice of blue-ribbon pie as well.

For quite some time after *Cafe Indiana* appeared on bookstore shelves, Joanne contemplated a cookbook based on the best-selling, everyday dishes, blue plate specials, and lunch buffet favorites from cafes around the state. Meat loaf, swiss steak, chicken and noodles or dumplings, biscuits and gravy. Hearty chili, classic salads, a few ethnic specialties. And, of course, pie and cobbler. You couldn't have a Hoosier cookbook without plenty of these.

Yes, there were lots of possibilities. But would the cafe owners Joanne wrote about in *Cafe Indiana* part with their recipes?

Once Jolene, a food writer for the *Indianapolis Star*, a native Hoosier, and the mom of three willing taste-testers, was on board, requests for recipes were mailed out to cafe owners. Some responded enthusiastically and quickly, mailing back instructions for everything from family favorites to a customer's creation that had become a local hit. Owners also submitted recipes for Joanne's special requests, often something she had eaten or a dish with an interesting story behind it.

The recipe collection steadily grew, but even so, Joanne had to do some convincing, talking cooks and cafe owners into sharing recipes for the quintessential Hoosier eats we couldn't do without. Denoted by ⬛, these menu items are identified over and over again by cafe owners and customers as top sellers and favorite choices. With a few of our own recipes thrown in to fill in the gaps, we finally rounded out the list of must-have dishes.

What we ended up with is pure Hoosier, a collection of recipes that does what few cookbooks do. It shows what people really cook and love to eat, day after day and week after week. *Cafe Indiana Cookbook* takes readers to Main Street, gets them a table at the local cafe, and hands them a menu of hearty home cooking.

"What people eat is not well documented," writes food writer Mark Kurlansky in *The Food of a Younger Land*. "Food writers prefer to focus on fashionable, expensive restaurants whose creative dishes reflect little of what most people are eating. We know everything about Paris restaurants but nothing about what Parisians eat. We know little about what Americans eat and less about what they ate."

Cafe Indiana Cookbook is about well-loved traditional food—comfort food, farm food, heartland cooking, food like Grandma used to make—that is time tested and community based, food that defines our collective Hoosier heritage and instills a sense of belonging and place that is often deeply personal and deeply emotional. Much of cafe food is edible folk art, and the cafe owners and cooks who prepare it are, according to Jane and Michael Stern of *Roadfood* fame, humble folk artists carrying on a precious cultural heritage.

Indiana's food traditions have been shaped—and continue to be shaped—by environment, climate, and history. The sandy prairies of northern Indiana give us blueberries and mint, for example, while the southern hills and hollers provide the fall persimmons that we make into pudding.

By history we mean the cultural heritage of Indiana's Anglo-European settlers. (Native American food traditions are not represented in today's small-town cafes.) The pioneers from the Midwest, Appalachian, and mid-Atlantic culture regions made a deep and lasting imprint on Hoosier culinary traditions. The influence of immigrants is also felt, especially the Germans who settled the Hoosier state in large numbers beginning in the 1830s, as well as those of Eastern European descent who peopled the industrial northwest and the Swiss Mennonites and Amish in the northeast, where the influence of Pennsylvania Dutch traditions is still found. The ethnic specialties of more recent immigrants—Mexicans, Asians, Africans—can make for surprising additions to Main Street menus, proving that Indiana's food traditions, despite their stubbornly conservative nature, are far from static.

We often hear that no one cooks anymore, that no one has time to make breakfast or bake a pie and, what's worse, that no one cares. But that's just not the case. Here in Indiana, we still file into the hometown restaurant on Sundays after church for fried chicken and dressing, mashed potatoes and gravy, and a slice of pie. We take our favorite covered dishes to family reunions, church pitch-ins, office potlucks, and carry-in dinners—and we're still happy and flattered when asked for a recipe. We may take a few more shortcuts today than Grandma did years ago. We may use Crockpots and convenience foods. But we still appreciate a home-cooked meal, maybe more so today in our admittedly fast-paced world than ever before.

The truth is, old-fashioned real food is alive and well in Indiana's small-town cafes. It's what Hoosiers eat. It's what Hoosiers like. It's what you'll find on the following pages. This is honest home cooking, straight from Main Street, from the cafe cooks and restaurant owners who know what their customers want.

In *Cafe Indiana Cookbook*, the meat loaf tastes just the way you remember it—hearty, filling, and flavorful. The french toast is still as sweet and satisfying, and the bread pudding still as rich and comforting as any you've ever had.

These recipes aren't dolled up with gourmet touches or hard-to-find ingredients, partly because these classic dishes don't really need any embellishments. But it's also because this cookbook isn't our interpretation of Indiana cafe fare. It's not a collection of Joanne's favorite pies or Jolene's best soups. Sure, we've found our favorites along the way. But this collection isn't about us.

It's about Indiana's cafes and the great food and great folks you'll find there. The recipes were graciously provided by cafe owners around the state, and we present them to you pretty much as we got them.

Oh, we've adjusted the quantities because not many home cooks need to make fifteen pounds of meat loaf. This means you should keep an eye on the varying quantities, which range from a single serving to servings of eight or more that could mean leftovers—though we doubt you'll mind enjoying many dishes a second time. We've also offered a few suggestions here and there for spicing things up a bit.

What you'll find in *Cafe Indiana Cookbook* is a satisfying menu of Hoosier home cooking. So, please, pass the pie. Let's eat.

Acknowledgments

Thank you to all the friends and family members, especially John, Aaron, Adam, and Jane, who served as tasters and were always game to sample yet another recipe.—J.K.

Appreciation and gratitude to the cafe owners, cooks, employees, and customers who provided recipes, answered my many questions, and carry on Indiana's food traditions and strengthen and sustain their communities. My friend and colleague Jon Kay, director of Traditional Arts Indiana, the state folk arts program, offered gentle direction and redirection when sought.—J.S.

CAFE OWNERS/CONTRIBUTORS

Daniel Alemu, Daniel's Ligonier Cafe, Ligonier; Ann Cain, Wolcott Theatre Cafe, Wolcott; Barbara Chambers and Jim Chambers, Chambers Smorgasbord, Spencer; Roger and Dawn Christman, Sue Christman, and Judy May, Old School Cafe, Pleasant; Janet and Ken Delaney, Janet's Kitchen, Rensselaer; Julie Fischer, Julie's Tell Street Cafe, Tell City; Liz Freeland, Liz's Country Cafe, North Salem; Floyd and Donna Friend, Gosport Diner, Gosport; Pieternella "Nel" Geurs, Nel's Cafe, Ossian; Bobbie Jo Hart and Bertha Burton, Bobbie Jo's Diner, Edinburgh; Penny Hawkins, Baby Boomers Cafe, Hamilton; Martha "Marty" and Bart Huffman, Marty's Bluebird Cafe, Laketon; Jackie and Merle Ingle, Jackie's Family Restaurant, Gas City; Karen Iovino and Vera Gouker, Hilltop Restaurant, Lakeville; Darrel and Betty Jenkins, Windell's Cafe, Dale; Sharon and Roger LeFever and Saundra and Keith Minger, Palmer House, Berne; Susie Mahler, Wendy Van Horn, and Ron Bowers, Cafe Max, Culver; Debbie Montgomery, Velma's Diner, Shoals; Lanny and Lois Pickett, Newberry Cafe, Newberry; Vicky and David Pingel, Vicky's Restaurant, Winamac; Tony and Linda Shuman, Highway 341 Country Cafe, Wallace; Don Storie, Chuck Storie, and Beth Storie-Sanders, Storie's Restaurant, Greensburg; and Candy and Alan Krull and Marsha Thomas, Corner Cafe, Wakarusa.

ONE

~ ~ ~

Breakfast

Sausage Gravy ⬧

CORNER CAFE, WAKARUSA
Candy and Alan Krull

Biscuits topped with sausage gravy is an Indiana cafe staple. "I love it," says cook Marsha Thomas, adding a rueful "I wish I didn't." Marsha uses a mild, fresh sausage made at John's Butcher Shop in Nappanee (see sidebar) and adds a bit of sage. Choose a mild or medium-spiced breakfast sausage for this cafe classic. For biscuit recipes, see pages 96 and 97.

Marsha operated the Corner Cafe in Nappanee from 1997 until it closed in September 2009. It wasn't long before her daughter Candy Krull proposed reopening in nearby Wakarusa, saying, "If you cook, I'll run the restaurant." The new and improved Corner Cafe welcomed its former customers, and a lot of new ones, too, on January 1, 2010. Were they ever glad to be back!

> 1 **pound pork sausage**
> ½ **teaspoon onion salt**
> **pepper to taste**
> ¾ **teaspoon sage**
> ½ **cup flour**
> 1½ **cups hot water**
> 2½ **cups milk**
> 1 **tablespoon butter**

Brown sausage with onion salt and pepper in a large, heavy skillet over medium heat, stirring well to break up sausage; add sage. Sprinkle flour over browned sausage. Cook, stirring, until flour is absorbed.

Slowly stir in water and milk. Cook, stirring occasionally, until gravy comes to a boil. Stir in butter. Season to taste with salt and pepper if needed. Serve over biscuits. Serves 4.

Neighbor to Neighbor

When Marsha Thomas runs low on meat at the Corner Cafe, she calls in an order to John's Butcher Shop in Nappanee. Then she'll stop by to pick it up or have it delivered. "Marsha has been ordering from us for so long that we know just what and how much she needs," says Nancy Miller, who owns the shop with her husband, Russell.

The hometown fresh meat market was begun in 1941 by Nancy's grandfather Earl Nunemaker, who was followed by her father, John Price. Not long after John retired and the Millers took over, Russell abandoned his given name for the eponymous John. "Everyone who came in asked for John," Nancy says.

Earl Nunemaker got his start in the frozen food plant business, building lockers at a time when most people didn't have a home freezer. As time went on, he opened a retail meat counter and then added processing. "An Amish gentleman south of town raises most of our beef for us, and we buy hogs from the sale barn," says Nancy. Today the Millers also maintain a strong wholesale business, providing quality meats to restaurants like the Corner Cafe.

On a daily basis, John's Butcher Shop is filled with steaks, roasts, pork chops, and chicken, and a variety of sausages, including bratwurst, Polish, and hot Italian. Other signature items include hickory-smoked bacon, seasoned prime rib, sausages, homemade deli salads, and cracklin's, or pork rinds, as soft as a puff.

At the Corner Cafe, Marsha Thomas prefers the Millers' lightly seasoned pork sausage—what she calls salt and pepper sausage—for biscuits and gravy. "A lot of my customers are older and don't like a lot of spice," she says. She buys fresh pork tenderloin run through a mechanical tenderizer for her breaded tenderloin sandwiches. During Nappanee's annual Apple Festival, she serves apple sausage, a specialty at John's Butcher Shop. "It's a fresh pork sausage made with sweet applesauce, brown sugar, and cinnamon. We have it all the time, but it's especially popular during the festival," Nancy says. —J.S.

Stuffed French Toast

HILLTOP RESTAURANT, LAKEVILLE

Vera Gouker and Karen Iovino

The Hilltop's delicious stuffed french toast is made extra special with the easy orange sauce topping. Don't skip the sprinkling of fresh blueberries in season. Top with thawed frozen blueberries if fresh are unavailable.

- $\frac{1}{2}$ **cup sugar**
- 2 **tablespoons cornstarch**
- **pinch salt**
- 2 **cups orange juice**
- 1 **(8-ounce) package cream cheese**
- $\frac{1}{4}$ **cup sugar**
- 1 **(8-ounce) can crushed pineapple, undrained**
- 1 **loaf french or italian bread**
- 2 **cups milk**
- 4 **eggs**
- $\frac{1}{2}$ **teaspoon vanilla extract**
- $\frac{1}{4}$ **teaspoon cinnamon**
- 1 **tablespoon butter**
- $\frac{1}{2}$ **cup fresh blueberries**

Stir together sugar, cornstarch, and salt in a medium saucepan. Add orange juice and cook over medium heat, stirring constantly, until mixture thickens and boils. Boil, stirring, for 1 minute; set aside.

Mix cream cheese and sugar with an electric mixer; stir in pineapple.

Cut bread on the diagonal into 8 slices, each about 1-inch thick; cut a slit into the side of each slice to form a pocket. Fill each pocket with about 2 tablespoons of cream cheese mixture.

Stir together milk, eggs, vanilla, and cinnamon.

Heat griddle or nonstick skillet over medium-high heat; melt butter. Dip each slice of bread into milk and egg mixture; place on heated griddle or skillet. Cook, turning once, until golden brown on each side.

Top with orange sauce and a sprinkling of blueberries. Serves 4.

Sinful French Toast

Cafe Max, Culver

Susie Mahler

This super-rich version of french toast starts with fresh-baked cinnamon rolls slathered in frosting. "It is an unbelievable draw," says the cafe's assistant manager, Wendy Van Horn. "We have several groups that ride their bikes every weekend from the neighboring town fifteen miles away just to eat a breakfast with Sinful French Toast." Try using cinnamon rolls made from the recipe on page 8.

- **4 prepared cinnamon rolls**
- **4 tablespoons butter, at room temperature**
- **1½ cups powdered sugar**
- **4 eggs**
- **1 cup milk**
- **¼ teaspoon cinnamon**
- **½ teaspoon vanilla extract**
- **1 tablespoon butter**

Sliced prepared cinnamon rolls horizontally. Cream together butter and powdered sugar, gradually adding powdered sugar until it forms a stiff mixture. Generously frost the uncut sides of each cinnamon roll.

Stir together eggs, milk, cinnamon, and vanilla.

Melt butter on a griddle or large nonstick skillet over medium heat. Dip sliced and frosted rolls into egg and milk mixture; place frosted side up on heated griddle. Cook until bottom side is browned, about 2 minutes.

Turn over and cook the frosted side, watching carefully so as not to burn frosting, just until frosting caramelizes, about 1 minute. Carefully remove from heat; place on plates frosted sides up. Serve with butter and syrup. Serves 4.

Banana Caramel Nut French Toast

Marty's Bluebird Cafe, Laketon

Martha "Marty" and Bart Huffman

This indulgent breakfast treat is a popular weekend special. "People love it," Marty says. It's also great made with croissants instead of Texas toast.

- **2 cups milk**
- **4 eggs**
- **½ teaspoon vanilla extract**
- **¼ teaspoon cinnamon**
- **1 tablespoon butter**
- **8 slices Texas toast-style thick-cut bread**
- **2 bananas, sliced**
- **¼ cup caramel sauce**
- **whipped cream and chopped pecans, for garnish**

Stir together milk, eggs, vanilla, and cinnamon. Heat griddle or non-stick skillet; melt butter. Dip bread in milk and egg mixture and cook in batches on griddle or in skillet until golden brown on both sides, turning once.

Place two slices on each plate; top evenly with sliced bananas. Drizzle each serving with 1 tablespoon caramel sauce. Garnish with whipped cream and chopped pecans. Serves 4.

Gingerbread French Toast

Marty's Bluebird Cafe, Laketon
Martha "Marty" and Bart Huffman

The batter for this variation on a classic uses fragrant gingerbread spices such as cinnamon, ginger, cloves, and nutmeg. Marty makes this with croissants, but you can use any type of thick-cut bread.

3	**cups milk**
6	**eggs**
1	**cup sugar**
1	**teaspoon cinnamon**
1	**teaspoon ground ginger**
½	**teaspoon ground cloves**
½	**teaspoon ground nutmeg**
6	**croissants**
1 to 2	**tablespoons butter**
	maple syrup

Stir together milk, eggs, sugar, and spices. Cut croissants in half lengthwise. Heat griddle or nonstick skillet over medium heat; melt 1 tablespoon butter. Dip croissant slices in milk and egg mixture. Cook on griddle or in skillet in batches, adding more butter when necessary, until golden brown on each side, turning once. Serve topped with maple syrup. Serves 6.

Cinnamon Rolls with Caramel Icing

CORNER CAFE, WAKARUSA
Candy and Alan Krull

Don't hesitate to try these terrific cinnamon rolls. The dough is easy to handle, and when you make them yourself, you can add all the cinnamon-and-sugar filling that you want. We suggest that you don't skimp.

2 packages dry yeast
½ cup warm water
½ cup milk
2 teaspoons salt
½ cup sugar
½ cup butter
3 eggs, beaten
6 cups flour, divided
½ cup butter, melted
1 cup brown sugar
2 tablespoons cinnamon, or to taste

Add yeast to warm water and let stand 5 minutes.

Heat milk until warm but not simmering; stir in salt, sugar, and butter. Remove from heat and set aside. In a large mixing bowl, combine yeast with milk mixture. Add eggs and 3 cups of the flour; mix well. Add remaining flour. Place bowl in draft-free area and cover with clean kitchen towel; let rise until dough doubles in size, about an hour.

Punch down dough. Divide in half. On a floured surface, roll dough into a rectangle (about 10-by-15 inches). Spread with half of melted butter. Combine brown sugar and cinnamon and sprinkle half of mixture over dough. Roll up lengthwise into logs. Repeat with remaining dough. Using bread knife or string, cut logs into ¾- to 1-inch slices. Place slices on lightly greased baking sheets and allow to rise about an hour. Bake at 350 degrees for 15 to 20 minutes until light brown. Cool briefly and drizzle with caramel icing (recipe follows). Makes 2 dozen.

Caramel Icing

2 cups brown sugar
1 cup butter
1 cup half-and-half
   powdered sugar

Combine first three ingredients in medium saucepan and cook over medium heat, stirring, until sugar is dissolved. Add powdered sugar, 1 tablespoon at a time, until icing reaches desired consistency. Drizzle over cinnamon rolls.

Eier Datch (Egg Pancakes)

PALMER HOUSE, BERNE

Sharon and Roger LeFever and Saundra and Keith Minger

This recipe of Swiss heritage results in light, thin pancakes that are spread with apple butter (a recipe is found on page 98), rolled up, and served with warm maple syrup. Although thicker than crepes, they are also excellent spread with jam, folded, and served like a dessert crepe with fresh berries and a sprinkling of powdered sugar.

**   4 eggs**
1½ cups milk
**   1 cup flour**
**   ½ teaspoon salt**
      generous pinch baking powder
**   4 teaspoons butter, divided**
      apple butter and maple syrup to serve

Beat eggs slightly; add to milk, stirring to combine. Mix together flour, salt, and baking powder; add egg mixture, stirring just until dry ingredients are moistened. Batter will be thin.

For each pancake, melt 1 teaspoon butter in large nonstick skillet over medium-high heat. Pour about ¾ cup of the batter into skillet, tilting skillet so batter evenly covers the bottom. Cook until middle is just set and edges are dry. Carefully slide large spatula under pancake and flip over; cook other side until lightly browned. Place on plate; spread with apple butter, roll up, and serve with warm maple syrup. Serves 4.

Gypsy Omelet

WOLCOTT THEATRE CAFE, WOLCOTT
Ann Cain

This over-the-top omelet combines all the classic flavors. The dish, which easily serves two or more, "is not for the fainthearted," says Ann, "but worth the occasional splurge." You might try the sausage gravy recipe on page 2 for this belly buster.

> 1 **tablespoon cooking oil**
> 1 **cup shredded fresh or refrigerated hash browns (thawed, if frozen)**
> 1 **cup diced ham, crumbled sausage, and/or diced bacon**
> 1 **cup total diced green pepper, chopped onions, and sliced mushrooms**
> 1 **tablespoon butter**
> 4 **eggs, beaten**
> ½ **cup shredded cheddar cheese**
> 1 **cup sausage gravy, heated**

In a medium nonstick skillet, heat oil and cook hash browns until crisp; keep warm. In a separate skillet, cook meat with vegetables and mushrooms until meat is done and vegetables are tender; set aside.

In a large nonstick skillet, melt butter. Add eggs and cook, lifting edges and tilting pan to allow uncooked eggs to run under edges. Cook eggs just until set. Add meat and vegetables, sprinkle with cheese, and fold closed, cooking just until cheese melts. Slide omelet onto large plate. Cover with hash browns and pour warm gravy over all. Serves 2.

BREAKFAST IS BIG IN INDIANA

At home, breakfast for me is a light snack and a cup of coffee with a quick read of the daily newspaper. I'm generally in a rush to get the day started and unwilling to spend time cooking or washing dirty dishes. Yet I know this is not par for the course, especially on a Saturday in any of the state's small-town cafes, where breakfast is big (make that BIG), especially with local men and vacationers.

Cafe owners repeatedly told me that breakfast is their busiest meal of the day—both in terms of a morning meal and in breakfast-type foods ordered any time of day. Saturdays were frequently identified as the busiest day of the week, due in most part to the heavy breakfast traffic.

"Breakfast has become a bigger deal in the past few years," notes Marsha Thomas of the Corner Cafe in Wakarusa. "The men'll pull the tables together and sit for hours. Every morning we have the same coffee guys at the front table. They're waiting every day at five 'til six before we even open." It's often over breakfast that local residents plan the annual festival, organize builds for Habitat for Humanity, and lay out a strategy for building a community center or new fire station. It's also where local contractors line up the day's work on cell phones, retired gents solve the problems of the world, and farmers discuss their progress in the fields and the price of corn. The atmosphere is chummy and clubby, not unlike the fellowship at the Legion hall or VFW post.

Whether they're heading off to work or spending another day of retirement around the house or on the golf course or lake, men stick pretty close to a reasonable diet during the work week—say, a fried egg or two with a side of toast, potatoes, and bacon washed down with bottomless cups of coffee. On Saturdays, however, caution is thrown to the wind. That's when the orders for impressive pileups of hash browns, eggs, biscuits and gravy, and meat—sausage, bacon, ham, pork chops, steaks, corned beef hash, even country-fried steak and breaded pork tenderloins—go to and fro between the dining room and kitchen at a breakneck pace. Unlike Sunday mornings occupied with church going, Saturdays are relatively unstructured and free flowing, allowing time to splurge on eats and linger in conversation with family and friends.

To vacationers, breakfast is a decadent splurge, a languorous elongation of the morning. Vacation time is suspended and weightless, with no difference at all between Wednesday and Saturday. Any day—and any time of day—is perfect for biscuits and gravy, omelets, fried potatoes, cinnamon rolls, plate-sized pancakes, and glammed-up french toast, all eaten in sizeable portions.

Compared with local men and vacationers, local women tend to be nibblers. An order of toast with tea, a pancake with a single egg over easy, or a bowl of oatmeal is about all they need to start their day. It's quite rare for a woman to breakfast alone, slightly more common for a pair to breakfast together, more common yet for a husband and wife. Groups of women are not often seen in small-town cafes, unless they are on an outing with fellow Red Hatters, church members, or other social clubs. If they are, you'll see a lot of cross-plate sharing going on. —J.S., adapted from *Cafe Wisconsin Cookbook*

The Obamalet

HILLTOP RESTAURANT, LAKEVILLE

Vera Gouker and Karen Iovino

Go green with the Obamalet, a hearty, slightly spicy way to serve up eggs. Plenty of spinach gives this light-textured concoction a definite green hue, while pepper jack cheese adds punch to this version of the breakfast classic.

2 or 3 slices bacon, chopped
1 tablespoon chopped onions
¼ cup sliced mushrooms
2 eggs
¼ cup frozen spinach, thawed and patted dry
1 tablespoon cream cheese
1 slice pepper jack cheese

In a medium nonstick pan, sauté bacon with onions and mushrooms. Beat eggs; stir in spinach. Spread egg mixture in skillet with bacon and onions and cook over medium-low heat until nearly set.

Spread cream cheese on slice of pepper jack cheese. Place cheese on omelet. Fold omelet over and cook just until cheese melts. Serves 1.

EGGS FOR BREAKFAST

Nothing is as basic as eggs for breakfast.

Nor so deceptively simple, as I inadvertently found out the first time I ordered a fried egg at a cafe counter as a novice adventure eater and the only out-of-towner in the place.

"How'd ya like that?" the waitress asked.

How indeed? Just how many ways could an egg be fried?

I described what I wanted: an egg with the white firm and tight, with no uncooked skim on top. Yolk set but not cooked through so my toast could mop up what flowed onto the plate when I broke the quivery globe with my fork.

"You want it sunny side up," she said.

As a well-seasoned trekker at my five hundredth cafe, I had eaten eggs prepared just about every way possible:

Sunny Side Up, basted: a fried egg whose yolk is cooked by spooning hot fat (preferably bacon drippings or butter) over it.

Sunny Side Up, steamed: a fried egg that is finished off by adding a little water to the grill before covering the egg with a saucepan lid. The steam sets the yolk.

Over Easy: a fried egg that is carefully flipped over so the yolk cooks but doesn't break. Specify whether you want the yolk runny or hard. A hard-cooked over-easy (sometimes called *over-hard*) is perfect between two halves of a biscuit (add sausage or bacon, with or without cheese), sandwiched between slices of bread (add fried bologna or not), or as topping for a burger.

Poached: an egg broken into and cooked in very hot water. Not a favorite of most cafe cooks because of the extra care and time it requires. As kids, we called a poached egg on toast a "man on a raft."

Bird in a Nest or Toad in a Hole: a slice of bread, buttered on both sides, a silver dollar-size hole cut out of the middle. Break an egg into the hole and then fry the whole thing on a grill, flipping carefully to cook the other side. (Not to be confused with Marty Huffman's "World Famous" Bird's Nest featured on page 22.)

Scrambled: eggs whisked with a bit of milk so that the yolk and white intermingle, cooked on a grill. Try any variety of add-ins, including shredded cheddar, ham, corned beef hash, veggies, hash browns, you name it, to make what is known as a skillet, scramble, or haystack. Or, roll it with other ingredients into a tortilla for a breakfast burrito.

Omelet: eggs beaten with milk that are poured onto the grill or into a skillet or omelet pan, cooked until set, and then filled with an assortment of ingredients and folded over. There are cheese omelets, meat omelets, cheese and meat omelets, Denver omelets, Western omelets, Mexican omelets, and so on.

I never encountered soft-boiled eggs in their shells served for breakfast. However, their hard-boiled siblings are reserved for side dishes like potato salad, kidney bean salad, pickled beets and eggs, deviled eggs, and, of course, egg salad sandwiches.

Eggs are rarely served without toast and jelly—grape, strawberry, mixed fruit, apple, orange marmalade, and if you're lucky, apple butter in single-serving, foil-topped plastic tubs. Even with toast, a mere egg on a plate often appears pitifully forlorn.Cafe customers are creative accessorizers. Common accompaniments include bacon, ham, sausage, steak, pork chops, or corned beef hash and carb-laden biscuits and gravy, fried potatoes, and pancakes. —J.S., adapted from *Cafe Wisconsin Cookbook*

Fried Cornmeal Mush

This simple, filling dish was brought to Indiana by migrants from Appalachia, where cornmeal is used in many ways, and also from people of Pennsylvania Dutch heritage who moved into the northern part of the state. The recipe for this Hoosier breakfast selection commonly made with yellow rather than white cornmeal comes from Jolene's files.

> 1 cup cornmeal
> 1 cup cold water
> 1 teaspoon salt
> 1 teaspoon sugar (optional)
> 3 cups boiling water
>   oil, bacon fat, or sausage drippings

In a large saucepan, stir together the cornmeal, water, and salt and optional sugar. Slowly pour in the boiling water, stirring constantly. Heat to boiling, stirring constantly. Cover and boil for another 5 minutes, stirring frequently so clumps don't form. Pour into a buttered loaf pan and allow to set in a cool place overnight.

To prepare, remove loaf from pan and slice. Heat oil, fat, or drippings in a pan or griddle. Dip each slice in flour and fry, turning one time. Serve with butter and syrup, tomato gravy (see the recipe on page 103), apple butter, or jelly.

Baked Oats

CORNER CAFE, WAKARUSA
Candy and Alan Krull

Candy's mom, Marsha Thomas, makes a big batch of this lighter, drier version of oatmeal every day. "I have people call me to find out if there's any baked oats," she says. "If we're out, they won't come in until I've made a new pan." Most enjoy it topped with milk and brown sugar. For a real treat, try it with cream.

- 2 **eggs**
- ½ **cup sugar**
- ½ **cup cooking oil**
- 2 **teaspoons baking powder**
- 1 **cup milk**
- 3 **cups old-fashioned oats**
  honey for drizzling
  raisins, milk, and brown sugar (optional)

In a mixing bowl, beat eggs, sugar, oil, and baking powder for 3 minutes. Add milk and oats; mix well.

Pour into greased 8-inch square baking dish; drizzle with honey. Bake at 350 degrees for 30 minutes. Serve topped with raisins, milk, and brown sugar, if desired. Serves 4 to 6.

Fancy Oats

MARTY'S BLUEBIRD CAFE, LAKETON
Martha "Marty" and Bart Huffman

Jazz up traditional oatmeal with these popular add-ins. Marty and Bart came up with this variation of an old-fashioned standby at home, and now it's a cafe standard. "We hardly sell plain oats anymore," says Marty.

> 1 **serving oatmeal, prepared according to package directions**
> 1 **tablespoon each chopped walnuts, diced apricots, raisins and dried cranberries**
> 1 **tablespoon plain yogurt**
> ½ **teaspoon brown sugar**

Sprinkle prepared oatmeal with walnuts, apricots, raisins, and dried cranberries. Add yogurt; sprinkle with brown sugar. Serves 1.

High Octane Oatmeal

HILLTOP RESTAURANT, LAKEVILLE
Vera Gouker and Karen Iovino

This power-packed oatmeal offers protein, Omega 3s, and antioxidants—what more could you ask from breakfast? Karen buys whole-grain quinoa and grinds it in her coffee grinder but says, "The seed is round and very small. Maybe you don't need to grind it at all." Quinoa and ground flax can be found at natural foods stores and some larger supermarkets.

> 1 **serving oatmeal, prepared according to package directions**
> 3 **tablespoons ground quinoa**
> 3 **tablespoons ground flax**
> 2 **teaspoons sunflower seeds**
> **blueberries, raisins, dried cranberries, and banana slices, as desired**

To prepared oatmeal, add ground quinoa and ground flax, stirring to combine. Sprinkle with sunflower seeds. Top with blueberries, raisins, dried cranberries, and bananas slices to taste.

Bluebird Cafe Breakfast Burrito

MARTY'S BLUEBIRD CAFE, LAKETON
Martha "Marty" and Bart Huffman

Served on weekends, this tasty combo wraps up bacon, eggs, potatoes, and cheese in well-stuffed tortillas. For a slimmer serving, divide among more tortillas.

- **4 slices bacon**
- **1 cup fresh or refrigerated cubed potatoes with onions (thawed, if frozen)**
- **2 eggs**
- **2 10-inch flour tortillas**
- **¼ cup shredded cheddar**
- **2 tablespoons salsa, or to taste**

In medium skillet, brown bacon until crisp; drain and crumble when cool. In same skillet, cook cubed potatoes with onions according to package directions until browned. Add eggs to skillet, stirring until eggs are done.

Divide mixture evenly between tortillas; top evenly with cheese. Add 1 tablespoon salsa to each; roll up to serve. Serves 2.

Breakfast Burrito

JACKIE'S FAMILY RESTAURANT, GAS CITY
Jackie and Merle Ingle

Jackie's friend Gloria brought the idea of a breakfast burrito home from Florida. "You tell me what's in it, and I'll make it," Jackie promised. Since that first experiment, the burrito has earned a permanent place on the menu. "People are surprised at the size of it. They're expecting something smaller. One is a meal by itself," says Jackie.

> 1 tablespoon cooking oil
> 1 cup shredded fresh or refrigerated hash browns
>   (thawed, if frozen)
> ¼ cup diced onions
> ¼ cup chopped green pepper
> ¼ cup sliced mushrooms
> ¼ cup diced tomatoes
> ¼ cup chopped broccoli
> 1 cup diced ham, crumbled sausage, or chopped
>   bacon, cooked
> 1 egg
> ¼ cup shredded cheddar cheese
> 2 10-inch tortillas
>   sour cream and salsa, for garnish

Heat oil in medium nonstick skillet. Cook hash browns with onions, green pepper, mushrooms, tomatoes, and broccoli until vegetables are tender; add meat. Add egg, stirring until scrambled.

Place tortillas on plates; divide mixture evenly between tortillas. Carefully roll up; top evenly with cheese. Heat in microwave 30 seconds at a time until cheese melts. Top with sour cream and salsa, if desired. Serves 2.

John Markland

JACKIE'S FAMILY RESTAURANT, GAS CITY
Jackie and Merle Ingle

Invented by city worker John Markland, this meat-packed breakfast roll-up quickly caught on with Jackie's customers. "Other city employees will call and order the 'Markland Special,'" she says.

2 or 3 slices bacon, chopped
  ¼ cup diced onions
  ¼ cup chopped green pepper
  ¼ cup diced tomatoes
  ¼ cup crumbled sausage, cooked
  ¼ cup diced ham
  1 beaten egg
  ¼ cup shredded cheddar cheese
  2 10-inch tortillas

In a medium nonstick skillet, cooked the chopped bacon with onions, green pepper, and tomatoes over medium heat. Add cooked sausage and diced ham. Add beaten egg, stirring until egg is done. Remove from heat, top mixture with shredded cheese, and cover skillet to allow cheese to melt. Distribute evenly between tortillas, rolling up to serve. Serves 2.

GOT GOETTA?

For many folks like Sue Christman at the Old School Cafe in Pleasant, the Saturday morning start-up would be a fizzle without their favorite goetta, a soft sausage made of pork, beef, steel-cut oats, and spices. You'll find goetta in only a handful of eateries, and only in southeastern Indiana, where immigrants from northwestern Germany established tight-knit communities that carried on Old World traditions that linger yet today. As a girl growing up in Hanover, Indiana, Sue's family enjoyed the goetta made by their next-door neighbors at hog-butchering time.

Today, Glier's in Covington, Kentucky, is the world's largest producer of goetta. Some one million pounds are made annually, with 99 percent bought and consumed within the regional Cincinnati area. Goetta has been serious business since the Glier family rolled out its first one-pound chub in 1946, but that doesn't mean they take themselves too seriously. In nearby Newport, the annual Goettafest held every August celebrates the porky peculiarity with tent after tent of all things goetta, including goetta

MAKE MINE CRISPY

Whether served crispy, covered with onions, or smothered with cheese, hash browns are a quintessential cafe side. But how to recreate that cafe classic at home?

After testing recipes for the Chambers Special, the Gypsy Omelet, a hash brown casserole, breakfast burritos, and the Bluebird Cafe's World Famous Bird's Nest, several things became clear.

First of all, when it comes to hash browns, fresh beats frozen anytime. Oh, the frozen patties are easy enough to handle, but it's tough to break apart frozen shredded hash browns—and even tougher to get them to brown up nicely.

But that doesn't mean you have to peel and shred potatoes just to enjoy a side of hash browns for breakfast. I was pleased to find in the refrigerated section of the supermarket packages of fresh—not frozen—hash browns.

(continued on facing page)

burgers, pizza, nachos, egg rolls, jambalaya, even goetta fudge brownies. A popular contest caters to clever cooks, like those who tuck goetta into wonton wrappers and sauce it up as *spagoetta*. The eating at Goettafest is mighty fine, but my favorite thing is the goetta vending machines. Put in some bills, push a button, and kawoomp! Out falls a frozen chub to tote home.

Back at the Old School Cafe, goetta is served in its simplest, unadulterated form. A one-pound roll is cut into ½-inch slices, sizzled on the hot grill until brown and crispy, and served alongside eggs, pancakes, french toast, or potatoes. Some like it plain, some top it with syrup, and others dredge it in the liquid yolk of their eggs.

Take inspiration from Goettafest, and experiment with new ways of using the old goetta. How about substituting it for sausage in the breakfast hash browns, burritos, and omelets in this chapter? Or how about goetta and gravy over biscuits or toast?

I have found goetta at stores in Madison, Indiana. Or, you can order goetta from Glier's—or plan your visit to Goettafest—at http://www.goetta.com/en/goettafest. —J.S.

Hash Brown Casserole

CHAMBERS SMORGASBORD, SPENCER
Barbara Chambers and Jim Chambers

This hearty option found a place on the menu after customers asked owner Barbara Chambers's late husband, Bob, for the combo that he often made for himself. It is served with fried biscuits and homemade apple butter, a unique southern Indiana pairing. For a recipe for each, see pages 96–98.

> 2 frozen hash brown patties
> 1 tablespoon cooking oil
> ¼ cup diced green pepper
> ¼ cup chopped onions
> ¼ cup sliced mushrooms
> ½ cup diced ham, crumbled sausage, or chopped bacon, cooked
> 1 slice American or Swiss cheese

Cook hash browns in medium nonstick skillet according to package directions; keep warm.

Heat oil in medium skillet; sauté green pepper, onions, and mushrooms until onions are soft and translucent and peppers are tender. Top cooked hash browns with sautéed vegetables and cooked meat.

Top with slice of cheese; cover skillet and cook over medium-low heat just until cheese melts. Serves 1.

Chambers Special

CHAMBERS SMORGASBORD, SPENCER

Barbara Chambers and Jim Chambers

"Breakfast anytime" at Chambers, a half block off the square in downtown Spencer, often means this popular dish, created by founder Bob Chambers, as a tasty way to combine eggs, potatoes, and cheese.

- 1 **cup fresh or refrigerated hash browns (thawed, if frozen)**
- 2 **eggs**
- 2 **teaspoons cooking oil**
- 2 **slices American cheese**
- ½ **cup diced ham, crumbled sausage, or chopped bacon, cooked**

Cook hash browns according to package directions; keep warm.

In a small nonstick skillet, fry eggs in oil to desired doneness.

Top hash browns with 1 slice cheese, cooked meat, and second slice of cheese. Slide cooked eggs on top of cheese. Serves 1.

(continued from facing page)

Not only are these easier to measure than the frozen variety, but there's no melting ice to deal with, one key to producing those coveted crispy edges.

For best results, cook fresh or refrigerated hash browns in a nonstick skillet or on a griddle with a bit of cooking oil over fairly high heat. Resist the temptation to stir them around too much; allow hash browns to begin to crisp up on the bottom before carefully flipping portions over. —J.K.

"World Famous" Bird's Nest

Marty's Bluebird Cafe, Laketon
Martha "Marty" and Bart Huffman

This breakfast hot seller is a perfect fit—"It looks like a bird's nest with eggs," says Marty—for this restaurant decorated with you guessed it. "Anything with a bluebird theme, we collect," Marty says. "We came across a Bluebird Cafe in southern Indiana, and I thought if I'd ever have a cafe of my own, that's what I'd do. . . . There's always room for more!"

> 2 **pieces bacon**
> 1 **cup fresh or refrigerated hash browns (thawed, if frozen)**
> ¼ **cup chopped green pepper**
> ¼ **cup chopped onion**
> ¼ **cup sliced mushrooms**
> 2 **eggs**
> ¼ **cup shredded cheddar**

In a medium skillet, cook bacon; drain and crumble when cool.

In same skillet, cook hash browns with green pepper, onion, and mushrooms until browned. Carefully add eggs, one at a time; cover and cook until eggs are white and yolks are cooked to desired doneness. Top with cheese and crumbled bacon. Serves 1.

TWO

~ ~ ~

Daily Specials

Meat Loaf

CHAMBERS SMORGASBORD, SPENCER
Barbara Chambers and Jim Chambers

Barbara doesn't recall when or where she got the recipe for this tasty meat loaf, but the restaurant has offered it for more than thirty-five years. "We serve meat loaf on Thursdays for lunch," she says. "It is a popular menu item on our buffet." Leftovers make great sandwiches.

$2\frac{1}{2}$ **pounds ground beef**
$1\frac{1}{4}$ **cups quick-cooking oats**
2   **eggs, beaten**
$1\frac{3}{4}$ **cups tomato juice**
1   **tablespoon dried onion**
$1\frac{1}{2}$ **teaspoons salt**
$\frac{1}{2}$ **teaspoon pepper**
   ketchup

In a large bowl, combine all ingredients except ketchup, mixing well. Pat into loaf pan (will fill 9-by-5-by-3-inch standard-size pan); top with ketchup. Bake for 2 hours at 350 degrees, checking during last half hour to be sure ketchup topping does not begin to brown (cover with foil if necessary). Allow to cool for a few minutes, then carefully remove loaf from pan and cut into slices. Serves 8.

Swiss Steak #1

CHAMBERS SMORGASBORD, SPENCER
Barbara Chambers and Jim Chambers

The recipe for this hearty version of swiss steak came from Barbara's mother-in-law, who with her husband operated the original Chambers restaurant outside of McCormick's Creek State Park in the 1950s. "It's very popular with our customers," Barbara says of the "Sunday only" special that has been served for over thirty years.

- ¼ **cup flour**
- ½ **teaspoon salt**
- ¼ **teaspoon pepper**
- 4 **cube steaks, about 1¼ pounds**
- 2 **tablespoons cooking oil**
- 6½ **cups water**
- ¼ **cup beef base**
- 2 **tablespoons cornstarch**
- 1 **cup sliced mushrooms**

Combine flour, salt, and pepper in a shallow bowl; dredge steaks in flour mixture. In a large, heavy skillet, heat oil and brown steaks on both sides.

In a large saucepan, combine 6 cups water with beef base, stirring to combine; bring to a boil. Dissolve cornstarch in remaining ½ cup water, stirring well. Add to boiling water and cook, stirring, until it begins to thicken; stir in mushrooms.

In a 9-by-13-inch baking pan, layer beef broth and steaks. Bake covered at 375 degrees for about 1 hour 30 minutes. Serves 4.

Cook's note: If additional gravy is needed, heat 1 cup water and 1 teaspoon beef base (or more to taste), stirring well. Add to gravy in pan, stirring to combine. Look for beef base, which is often used to add flavor and color, with the bullions and instant soups in most large supermarkets.

Doing the Math

Where do you start when translating a restaurant recipe for use in a home kitchen?

The first problem is often just getting something on paper. Many restaurant cooks have been serving up their specialties for so long that they don't use recipes. Like experienced home cooks, they simply add what is needed and cook until it's done.

But once you get them talking—and then turn their squirts of mustard and handfuls of flour into measurements—you've got something to work with.

Other recipes are more precise, which presents another type of challenge. Oh, it's not the ingredients that pose a problem—most cafe kitchens use common enough ingredients. It's just that they use so much of them.

When you're making eighty servings of swiss steak and cooking gravy by the gallon, you might not worry about precise measurements. But when you cut that down to four servings, every teaspoon counts.

It's not simply a matter of cutting amounts in half. When working with restaurant recipes, you often have to cut them in half, then in half again, and again after that. Barbara Chambers's swiss steaks, for example, needed yet another halving to get them down to a manageable 1¼ pounds.

Gravy proportions prove a bit more complicated. The ratio for reducing those steaks just didn't yield enough of the accompanying mushroom gravy. So it was back to the notepad for a little more figuring, then back to the stove for a little more tinkering.

When it comes to canned goods, we aren't surprised that cafe cooks aren't using typical 14.5-ounce cans from the supermarket shelf. Restaurants identify cans by numbers.

But just what is a No. 10 can of applesauce—and why would you need four of them?

Amounts sometimes vary of course, but a No. 10 can often contains about twelve cups. So what in the world would you make with forty-eight cups of applesauce and just three other ingredients? The folks at Chambers Smorgasbord in Spencer use that much applesauce—along with six tablespoons of cinnamon, six cups of brown sugar, and cinnamon red hot candies—to make an oven-baked apple butter that's served alongside the restaurant's classic fried biscuits (see pages 97 and 98).

It's an easy method, as long as you have a pan big enough to hold it all and the six or seven hours needed to bake it into a deep brown apple butter.

Luckily, it doesn't take nearly as long when you're using just one jar of applesauce. Yet it still results in a sweet, cinnamony spread that's perfect on your morning toast—as well as on those Hoosier fried biscuits. —J.K.

Swiss Steak #2

CAFE MAX, CULVER
Susie Mahler

It's no surprise that this recipe is a lunchtime favorite at Cafe Max. "Comfort food is what the cafe is all about," says assistant manager Wendy Van Horn. In the unlikely event that you have leftovers, they make a great starter for stew.

$\frac{1}{2}$ **cup flour**
$\frac{1}{2}$ **teaspoon salt**
$\frac{1}{4}$ **teaspoon pepper**
4 **cube steaks, about 1 $\frac{1}{2}$ pounds**
2 **tablespoons cooking oil**
1 or 2 **thinly sliced carrots**
1 **small onion, minced**
1 **rib celery, sliced**
1 **(14.5-ounce) can whole tomatoes**
4 **cups water**
4 **teaspoons beef base**

Combine flour, salt, and pepper. Dredge steaks in mixture. In a heavy skillet, heat oil and brown steaks on both sides; place steaks in 9-by-13-inch baking pan. Over steaks, place carrots, onion, celery, and tomatoes (with juice).

Stir together water and beef base; pour over steaks and vegetables in pan. Cover and bake at 350 degrees for about 1 hour 30 minutes.

Salisbury Steak

HIGHWAY 341 COUNTRY CAFE, WALLACE
Tony and Linda Shuman

These extra-hearty Salisbury steaks weigh in at a hefty ten ounces apiece when Tony makes them—and a full serving includes two. This version calls for patties that are somewhat smaller, if only to make them easier to handle when browning. Tony serves them with mashed potatoes, which we agree is the ideal accompaniment.

  20 saltine crackers, crushed
   2 eggs, beaten
  2¼ pounds ground chuck
      salt and pepper
   1 cup flour
   1 teaspoon seasoned salt
   2 tablespoons vegetable oil
   2 packages brown gravy mix
   1 can cream of mushroom soup

Stir together crushed saltines and beaten eggs. Mix into ground chuck; season with salt and pepper.

Shape meat mixture into 4 to 6 patties about ¼ inch thick and about 6 inches across.

Combine flour and seasoned salt in a shallow bowl; dredge patties in flour-salt mixture. Heat oil in large, heavy skillet and brown patties on both sides (patties are large, so use care in turning). Place in 9-by-13-inch baking dish. Prepare gravy mixes as directed; add undiluted cream of mushroom soup, stirring well. Pour over steaks. Cover and bake at 350 degrees about an hour. Serves 4 to 6.

Country-Fried Steak with Gravy

This is one of those dishes that we just had to include, even though it wasn't submitted by a cafe owner. Sometimes called chicken-fried steak, this is classic Hoosier cafe fare that is best served with mashed potatoes and creamy white gravy. In its preparation—pounding to tenderize and flatten the beef, coating with flour, and then frying— it is not too unlike the breaded pork tenderloin (see pages 70–75). While country-fried steak is traditionally a peppery dish, feel free to adjust the seasonings to taste.

- **4 cube steaks or 1 pound round steak cut into 4 pieces and pounded to about $\frac{1}{3}$-inch thick**
- **salt and pepper**
- **$\frac{1}{2}$ cup vegetable oil**
- **2 eggs beaten with 2 teaspoons milk**
- **$1\frac{1}{2}$ cups plus 3 tablespoons flour**
- **1 teaspoon pepper**
- **2 cups milk**

Season steaks with salt and pepper. Heat oil in a large, heavy cast-iron or stainless-steel skillet. Place the egg-milk mixture in a shallow dish. Place the $1\frac{1}{2}$ cups flour in a separate shallow dish; add 1 teaspoon pepper, stirring to combine.

Dredge steaks in the flour, then dip in egg mixture. Dredge again in the flour, shaking off any excess, before carefully placing steaks in the hot oil. Cook, turning once, until golden brown, about 3 minutes per side. Remove steaks and drain on paper towels.

Pour off all but about $\frac{1}{4}$ cup of the oil. Sprinkle the remaining 3 tablespoons of flour over the oil and cook over medium heat, stirring constantly for several minutes, scraping up the browned bits. Slowly add the milk, a little at a time, stirring constantly. Bring to a boil, then cook, stirring, until thickened, adding more milk or water to achieve desired thickness. Season gravy to taste with salt and plenty of pepper. Serve steaks covered with gravy. Serves 4.

Roast Beef Manhattan ⭑

Bobbie Jo's Diner, Edinburgh
Bobbie Jo Hart

Is there nothing quite so comforting as down-home farm food? Hot roast beef, rich gravy, mashed potatoes, and white bread served together on a single plate may well be the iconic blue plate diner special. Bertha Burton, queen of the kitchen at Bobbie Jo's Diner, has been pleasing folks with this Sunday dinner–quality dish for more than fifty years. In Edinburgh, Bertha is everyone's grandma, both sweet as pie and steadfast as the stars.

    3 pounds beef roast (such as top round or bottom
          sirloin)
       salt and pepper
    2 tablespoons cornstarch
    6 potatoes, peeled and cut into 1-inch cubes
   12 slices white sandwich bread

Preheat oven to 350 degrees. Season roast well with salt and pepper. Place in roasting pan; add enough water to come about halfway up meat. Roast, uncovered, until roast reaches desired level of doneness, about 1½ to 2 hours, adding more water if necessary. When done, remove from oven and let rest 15 minutes. Remove roast to another pan and, using forks, shred into small pieces.

While roast is baking, boil potatoes until tender. Drain, reserving some of the cooking water; return drained potatoes to hot pan, stirring to allow excess water to evaporate.

Mash potatoes with enough of the cooking water (or milk) to reach desired consistency; season with salt and pepper.

To make gravy, pour broth from roasting pan into saucepan, reserving ½ cup of broth. Bring broth to simmer over medium heat. Stir the cornstarch into the reserved ½ cup of broth, stirring well until combined. Slowly add to simmering broth, stirring until thickened. Season to taste with salt and pepper.

To assemble Manhattans, place 1 slice sandwich bread on each plate. Top with shredded roast beef and another slice of bread. Cut sandwich diagonally; place a scoop of mashed potatoes between halves and pour gravy over all. Serves 6.

Marty's Famous Potpie

MARTY'S BLUEBIRD CAFE, LAKETON

Martha "Mary" and Bart Huffman

This hearty and warming beef potpie smells great and tastes even better. "It sure is good," says Marty. "Customers love it." Feel free to top the filling with a homemade pie crust (see recipes on pages 108 and 109).

> **2** tablespoons cooking oil
> **1½–2** pounds stew beef
> salt and pepper to taste
> **2** packages brown gravy mix
> **2** (16-ounce) packages frozen mixed vegetables
> **1** package refrigerated pie crusts (2 crusts), at room temperature

In a large, heavy skillet, heat oil. Add stew beef and cook, stirring, until browned. Add gravy mixes and half the amount of water called for, stirring to combine; add additional water, if necessary, to reach desired thickness. Stir in vegetables.

Pour mixture into 9-by-13-inch baking dish. Unroll pie crusts and top beef and vegetable mixture with crusts, cutting crusts as necessary to fit. Bake at 350 degrees according to package directions until crusts are golden brown. Serves 6.

Jackie's Family Restaurant is identified by a large plastic sign with snap-in black letters topped by a row of white light bulbs. Three of the five light bulbs are lit, casting elongated white reflections on the glossy black pavement of the parking lot. With its rustic board covering and chunky boxed entrance, the building is more utilitarian than pretty—the kind of restaurant you would drive past without paying much notice. Inside, the walls are covered with wood-grain paneling and unpainted waferboard. Decorations are limited to a collection of golf clubs, framed prints, a Tiger Woods Wheaties box that reflects Merle Ingle's passion for the game, and a smattering of Elvis photos.

But look more closely. There are one, two, three, four, five, six calendars to help diners keep track of the months and days. Jackie is unfamiliar

(continued on facing page)

Pot Roast

JACKIE'S FAMILY RESTAURANT, GAS CITY
Jackie and Merle Ingle

This long-simmered pot roast is comfort food at its finest, especially when served alongside real mashed potatoes. Leftovers are perfect for two menu mainstays: Roast Beef Manhattan (see page 30) or beef and noodles (see page 33).

> 3- to 5-pound boneless pot roast
> salt and pepper
> 2 tablespoons vegetable oil
> 1 medium onion, chopped
> 2 ribs celery, chopped
> 1 tablespoon beef base dissolved in 1 cup water
> 2 teaspoons steak seasoning
> ¼ teaspoon garlic powder

Season roast with salt and pepper. In a deep, heavy skillet or dutch oven, heat vegetable oil over medium-high heat. Add the roast and brown on all sides. Add onions and celery. Add water with beef base. Sprinkle steak seasoning and garlic powder over all.

Add enough hot water to nearly cover the roast and bring to a boil. Reduce heat, cover, and simmer until tender, 2 to 4 hours, depending on thickness of roast, adding more water as needed to keep roast nearly covered. To serve, cut into pieces, spooning broth over the top. Serves 6 to 10.

Beef and Noodles 🌟

WINDELL'S CAFE, DALE
Betty and Darrel Jenkins

For a hearty, filling serving of comfort on a plate, beef and noodles fills the bill. This recipe is easy to adapt to individual tastes; add more or less vegetables as desired (toss in some frozen peas, for example, near the end of cooking time, or use pearl onions instead of chopped). It can also be made with leftover pot roast (see page 32) or homemade noodles such as those on the next page.

- 2 **pounds round steak**
- **salt and pepper**
- ¼ **cup flour**
- 2 **tablespoons vegetable oil**
- 4 **cups beef stock, divided**
- 2 **bay leaves**
- 1 **small onion, chopped**
- 2 **carrots, sliced**
- 1 **(8-ounce) package egg noodles**

Trim round steak and slice across the grain into bite-size pieces. Season well with salt and pepper and toss with flour.

In a large, heavy skillet, heat vegetable oil until hot. Add beef and sauté until browned, about 5 minutes. Add 1½ cups beef stock, stirring well and scraping up browned bits. Add bay leaves, onions, and carrots. Cover and simmer about 20 minutes, until beef and carrots are tender.

Add 2 cups stock, stirring well. Add egg noodles, stir well, and simmer until noodles are tender, adding additional stock if necessary. To thicken, stir 1 tablespoon flour into ¼ cup stock or water, stirring well to combine. Add to mixture in skillet and simmer, stirring, until thickened. Season well with salt and pepper. Serves 4 to 6.

(continued from facing page)

with William Least Heat-Moon's wall calendar method of rating cafes found in his American travelogue, *Blue Highways*. At the don't-bother-eating-here end of the scale are one-calendar cafes serving "preprocessed food assembled in New Jersey." At the other end are seven-calendar cafes, golden dreams of the past talked about fondly by old-time travelers and businessmen. She laughs when she realizes just one more calendar will elevate her restaurant to legendary status. "I guess we'd better find another one." —J.S., adapted from *Cafe Indiana*

Chicken and Noodles 🚩

JACKIE'S FAMILY RESTAURANT, GAS CITY
Jackie and Merle Ingle

This comforting dish may well be Hoosiers' most beloved. It is not, as some might think, simply a version of chicken noodle soup. Chicken and noodles, made with fresh, homemade noodles and plenty of chicken, is an entrée served on a plate, not in a bowl. Be sure to have some bread handy to sop up the broth, or serve it spooned over mashed potatoes.

> 3　**cups flour**
> ¼　**teaspoon salt**
> 4　**eggs**
> 　　**3-pound chicken, cut up, or pieces, such as breasts**
> 　　　**and thighs**
> 1　**tablespoon chicken base, or 1 bouillon cube**
> 　　　**(optional)**
> 　　**salt and pepper to taste**

Combine flour, salt, and eggs, stirring well to combine. If dough is too wet to roll out, add additional flour (if too dry, add another egg yolk). On a floured surface, roll out dough until thin (about ⅛ inch). Allow to dry for about an hour.

Meanwhile, place chicken in a large stockpot and cover with water; add chicken base or bouillon cube, if desired. Bring to a boil; cook at a gentle boil for about 45 minutes to an hour, adding more water if necessary. Remove chicken and debone, returning meat to pot.

Cut noodles into thin strips lengthwise; cut crosswise into pieces about 2 inches long. Return chicken to a simmer. Add noodles and cook, stirring occasionally, until noodles are done. Season to taste with salt and pepper. Serves 4 to 6.

Cook's note: Chicken base, often used to add flavor and color, is typically found with bouillon and instant soups in most supermarkets.

NOODLES VS. DUMPLINGS

Do you know about Indiana's Chicken and Noodle Line? It is impossible to locate on a map, but it cuts the state into north and south. In order to keep things neat, let's somewhat arbitrarily assign the title to U.S. 40—the National Road. Hoosiers living north of the Chicken and Noodle Line eat chicken and noodles. For those south of the Line, noodles become dumplings. You'll occasionally find noodles and dumplings in the other's territory, but you'll never find cafe owners claiming them to be best sellers on their menus.

Except at the former Chicken Inn in Mitchell, whose owners operated a same-named restaurant in Shelbyville, which, while admittedly not exactly north of the Chicken and Noodle Line, is close enough. While the two Chicken Inn menus were virtually the same at both locations, the Shelbyville folks eat chicken and noodles without squawking. In Mitchell, however, customers made it perfectly clear that they were the chicken and dumplings type. The owners compromised and served both.

As a transplant to Indiana from the Upper Midwest, I am intrigued that Hoosiers distinguish so closely between the two. To me, they seem darn near the same thing: chicken, unseasoned broth, and bits of simmered dough. In fact, many recipes for noodles and dumplings contain exactly the same ingredients. At the Chicken Inn in Mitchell, I had the unique opportunity to put the two head-to-head in a taste and texture test.

"You want a cup of chicken and noodles and a cup of chicken and dumplings?" asked my teenage server, her pen suspended quizzically above the order pad. She returned only a polite, vacant smile as I explained my mission to get to the bottom of the noodles-dumplings conundrum.

Hoosier noodles versus dumplings? I confess that I am able to distinguish only slight differences between the two, namely the shape and density of the simmered dough.

Common to the northern United States, noodles are made from rolled dough cut into narrow strips. If made with eggs, they tend to be more dense and chewy than those sans eggs, and they also have a lemony hue. Some recipes even call for the addition of yellow food coloring to punch up the appearance.

Rolled dumplings, on the other hand, are a tradition belonging to the southern United States. Like their northern cousins, dumplings also can be made with or without eggs. Unlike noodles, dumplings are cut into wide strips, squares, or triangles. In many families, "potpie" is the name

for both wide strips and the dish made with them. "Dog ear" often refers to square or triangular dumplings.

Dropped dumplings, too, come in northern and southern varieties. Made with leavening, Yankee dumplings are thick and fluffy and float on top of the broth. Dixie dumplings are noodlelike, tender and soft, and fall to the bottom of the pan while they cook in the broth.

Whether noodles or dumplings, Hoosiers agree on how to eat the chicken and beef varieties of this favorite dish. Plain is oh-so-good. Better is over a mound of mashed potatoes. Best is both stirred together with a fork. —J.S.

Chicken and Dumplings #1

JULIE'S TELL STREET CAFE, TELL CITY
Julie Fischer

Another homey dish, chicken and dumplings is, again, not a soup but rather a main dish, and a most popular one at that. "At the restaurant we have chicken and dumplings every Thursday and sometimes on our Friday night buffet," says Julie. "People get to asking, 'Isn't it about time you had chicken and dumplings again?'"

> 3 **pounds chicken pieces**
> 1 **tablespoon chicken base (optional)**
> ½ **cup margarine**
> ½ **cup milk**
> 3 **cups flour**
> 1 **egg**
>   **salt and pepper to taste**

Place chicken in a large stockpot and cover with water, adding chicken base if desired. Bring to a boil and cook for 45 minutes to an hour, adding water as necessary. Remove chicken and debone, returning meat to pot.

In a small saucepan, heat margarine and milk until margarine melts. Place flour in large bowl. Add milk mixture and egg, stirring well to combine.

On a floured surface, roll out dough to about ½-inch thick; cut into ½-inch squares. Return chicken to a boil; drop dumplings into boiling liquid and cook, covered, for 15 to 20 minutes. Season with salt and pepper to taste. Serves 4.

Chicken and Dumplings #2 🔖

WINDELL'S CAFE, DALE
Betty and Darrel Jenkins

If you're on your own and need a little love like Grandma used to make, take heart—this single serving of chicken and dumplings is just the thing. Leftover rotisserie chicken works great, but even the canned variety will do in a pinch.

- 1 **cup self-rising flour**
- 2 **tablespoons shortening**
- ⅓ **cup milk, plus more if necessary**
- 4 **cups chicken broth**
- 4 **ounces (about ½ cup) cooked chicken, diced**

Place flour in a bowl; make a well in the flour and add shortening. Cut shortening into flour until grainy. Add milk a little at a time, until dough begins to hold together. Turn out onto a floured surface and knead a few times, adding flour if dough is sticky. Roll out dough to about ½-inch thick and cut into evenly sized pieces.

Heat broth to boiling; add dumplings. Return to boiling; cover and reduce heat. Simmer 15 to 20 minutes until dumplings are tender. Add chicken and heat until chicken is warmed through. Serves 1.

IF THEY COME, YOU BUILD IT

When Darrel and Betty Jenkins bought Windell's Cafe in the tiny town of Dale in 1991, it consisted of a small block building seating no more than about forty-five people. As hometown heirs to Windell's nearly fifty-year legacy of ultragood home cooking, the Jenkinses were content to carry on the modest cafe's time-tested traditions. They catered to a local crowd and maintained a pretty low profile. "The main thing we tried to do was keep the same home cooking," Darrel says. In fact, many of the original recipes are still being used.

The tide unexpectedly changed in 1994. That's when a hungry writer for *Midwest Living* magazine in pursuit of great eating along America's interstates received a tip about the virtues of Windell's victuals from a semitruck driver. He came. He ate. From his Des Moines office, he called Darrel and Betty for an interview. "I wasn't too sure about that," Betty recalls, but she gamely answered his questions. And then he wrote, extolling the pleasure of Windell's chicken and dumplings and so-perfect pies. Others wishing to document Windell's magic quickly followed: newspaper

reporters from a three-state area, television news crews and WFYI's *Across Indiana*, even the nationally distributed cable Food Network.

"It was in the winter of 2004, and they came down from New York on a Sunday afternoon," Betty remembers. "We were so surprised because it was so cold and snowy; we thought they'd cancel. No one was here because the churches had all canceled their services. They were on a chicken theme and featured our chicken and dumplings. The show has been shown several times since then. I'm surprised at how many people say they've seen it. It's been good for business."

The media lit the way through the dining wilderness, inspiring legions of adventure eaters to trek to the Shrine of Home Cooking in little old Dale, Indiana. "It wasn't long before we started getting tour buses," Darrel remembers. "We had single stall bathrooms and would have forty to fifty people standing in line. We knew we had to do something when our employees had to go home to use the bathroom!"

The dramatic increase in customers necessitated an extensive remodeling. The Jenkinses enlarged the kitchen to three times its original size, expanded the dining room across a vacated alley, and added a public meeting room and two very large rest rooms. Addition of a buffet was another strategic response to the tremendous influx of out-of-area customers.

"We often wonder why we didn't just tear down the old building and build new," Darrel says. "It would have been a lot easier. . . . On the other hand, we could have kept our old building, not remodeled, and stayed out of debt. But we saw it as a service to the community to stay in business. It would be a very dark day in Dale if Windell's had closed." —J.S., adapted from *Cafe Indiana*

Pan-Fried Chicken

HIGHWAY 341 COUNTRY CAFE, WALLACE
Tony and Linda Shuman

Fried chicken is served with mashed potatoes and gravy for lunch on Sundays, says Tony, "and once in a while during the week to change things up." Tony uses extra-large chicken breasts; the bone-in variety with skin makes the most flavorful fried chicken. Or use thighs and drumsticks if you prefer dark meat.

- **4 large bone-in chicken breasts with skin (3½ to 4 pounds)**
- **2 cups flour**
- **2 teaspoons salt**
- **1 teaspoon pepper**
  vegetable oil for frying

Rinse and drain chicken. In a shallow bowl, combine flour, salt, and pepper. Dip damp chicken breasts into flour mixture, turning to coat well. Shake off excess; let coating dry.

Heat about ½ inch oil in a large, deep heavy skillet. Carefully place chicken in skillet. Cover and cook over medium-high for 10 minutes or until browned on the bottom (check after 5 minutes and reduce heat if pieces are browning too quickly). Use tongs to turn chicken over and cook, uncovered, 10 to 12 more minutes, until bottom side is well browned and an instant-read meat thermometer inserted into the thickest parts of chicken registers 165 to 170 degrees. Serves 4.

Chicken Livers

Windell's Cafe, Dale
Betty and Darrel Jenkins

Not everyone has a taste for livers and onions, it's true, but this once-common dish enjoys a pretty widespread popularity. Still, it isn't often that a whole family enjoys the distinctive flavor and texture of liver, so here is a one-person serving, just like you'd get at Windell's Cafe.

    8 to 10 livers (about 6 to 8 ounces)
½ cup flour
½ teaspoon salt
¼ teaspoon pepper
    oil for frying
2 strips bacon, chopped
1 thick slice onion, diced

Rinse livers under cold running water; drain. Combine flour, salt, and pepper. Dredge livers lightly in flour mixture. Heat oil; fry until livers are golden brown and cooked through. Set aside and drain.

In a medium skillet cook bacon and onions together until bacon is crisp and onions are tender. Add livers, stirring together until livers are hot. Serves 1.

Chicken in Apricot Sauce

Wolcott Theatre Cafe, Wolcott
Ann Cain

Ann says this easy dish is a "good fix-it-and-forget-it with staples that you have on hand." We have to agree. It's great for a busy weeknight meal.

8 chicken breasts
    salt and pepper
    splash of lemon juice
1 cup Thousand Island dressing
1½ cups apricot preserves
1 envelope Lipton onion soup mix
1 clove garlic, pressed

Place chicken in large baking dish. Sprinkle with salt, pepper, and lemon juice. Mix remaining ingredients and pour over chicken. Bake at 350 degrees for 1 hour. Serve over pasta or with steamed broccoli. Serves 8.

Ham Loaf

Wolcott Theatre Cafe, Wolcott
Ann Cain

"This is very much a local favorite," says Ann, who sometimes makes this flavorful recipe as balls instead of loaves. "It's even better as leftovers, if you have any."

  1 **pound ground ham**
$\frac{1}{2}$ **pound ground pork**
$\frac{1}{2}$ **pound ground beef**
$\frac{1}{4}$ **teaspoon pepper**
  1 **cup crushed saltines**
  1 **egg plus 1 egg yolk**
$\frac{1}{2}$ **cup milk**

Combine all ingredients in a large bowl; divide into 4 to 6 mini loaf pans. Bake at 350 degrees for about an hour, basting with sauce (recipe follows) every 20 minutes. Serves 4 to 6.

     Sauce for Ham Loaf
$\frac{3}{4}$ **cup brown sugar**
$\frac{1}{4}$ **cup ketchup**
$\frac{1}{4}$ **cup cider vinegar**
$\frac{1}{2}$ **teaspoon dry mustard**

In a small saucepan, mix ingredients and bring to a boil.

MOONLIGHTING

For six weeks beginning in the deep heat of July, Ann Cain entrusts the Wolcott Theatre Cafe, which she opened in 2004, to her employees and customers while she serves as hotelkeeper at the Fountain Park Chautauqua outside Remington. In 1893, a local banker envisioned bringing cultural and educational opportunities to area residents. Today Fountain Park is one of just three remaining, continuously operating Chautauqua parks in the United States.

With a trusted crew of local kids, Ann opens up the century-old, two-story hotel. Windows are thrown open to admit fresh breezes, cobwebs are swept away, and the kitchen is readied to serve the hundreds of Fountain Parkers who will pass through the dining room during the two-week Chautauqua season. All of this interrupts Ann's everyday life to such a degree that she questions whether it is worth it. "But then I think if everyone thought Park wasn't worth the effort, it wouldn't be here."

Fountain Park Chautauqua is a hard thing to describe to the uninitiated. It is a physical place that time forgot: a park anchored by the hotel and a 500-seat tabernacle and ringed by privately owned cottages, many in the same family for several generations. More importantly, it is a state of mind. It is a reunion of nuclear families and the extended Park family, a spirited embodiment of community volunteerism, a wholesome and genuine expression of love of God and country.

"When I tell people about Park, they ask me, 'What's there to do?' And I say nothing. There is nothing to do—no pool, no lake, no golf course—and they look at me like I'm crazy. That's the charm of Park. People have to entertain themselves. They visit, reconnect with friends, play lawn games. They just slow down and relax," Ann says.

But look closely: someone else's tireless work lurks behind that simplicity and ease. Ann and her team of kids—Tori, Noah, and Elijah Legler and nephew Dylan Cain—roll out of their hotel beds while it is still dark to prepare a hot breakfast for hotel guests and cottage residents, followed by the noon and evening meals. "It's a kid-powered kitchen except for me," Ann explains. With the exception of twelve-year-old Elijah, for whom the 2009 season was his first, the others have been together since Ann took over the hotel. "Noah came to me when he was eight," remembers Ann. "I looked down at him and said, 'Are you looking for your mom?' He said, 'No, I'm here to help.' And I thought, 'Okay.' The kids have grown up with it and it's now automatic. They just know what to do." The dining room itself is run by Ethan Thomas and Rachel Harper with help from local kids and others staying in campers and cottages.

Ann creates the menu for the two-week Park season, opting for "heart-land cooking" like ham loaf (Tori says it's the number one favorite), pot roast, mashed potatoes, and cobbler. "People don't get the opportunity to eat food like this much anymore," Ann explains. "We had this one little boy who came up to me in the lobby and said, 'Ma'am, that meat loaf was just awesome!'" Occasionally, one of the kitchen kids will suggest something new, or dig out a recipe from the hotel file that hasn't been made in years. The routine can be shaken up only slightly. "People don't want to see a lot of changes because they come here for the sameness."

A seventeen-year-old Tri-County High School basketball star, Noah has a gift for cooking that has matured under Ann's guidance and by watching cable cooking shows. "We call him Little E, after Emeril," Ann says, gesturing toward the kitchen. "Noah would be a rock star at this. He has the personality, the team mentality, and the work ethic, and he has a presence and a calmness that you don't see in the TV celebrity chefs."

After so many seasons together, Ann absolutely relies on the kids, who drive into town to buy the groceries, prepare an entire breakfast by themselves, and manage the kitchen so Ann can attend programs in the tabernacle and classes in the art building. "They laugh and remember when I wouldn't let them light the gas stove! I'm thankful that I've been here long enough to watch them claim ownership in the hotel and Fountain Park. They're so proud of the fact that they have made some people stand back and rethink kids today." —J.S.

PERKIER PATTIES

Do you prefer your salmon patties with a little more zing? A little more bite? Try one or more of the following suggestions, adjusting quantities as needed and mixing and matching to suit your taste:

Substitutions for the bread crumbs

- ½ cup Italian seasoned bread crumbs
- ½ cup quick-cooking oats
- 1 sleeve of saltines, crushed

Additions:

- 1 tablespoon lemon juice
- 1 to 1½ tablespoons Dijon-style mustard
- salt and pepper
- ½ cup chopped onion or green onion
- ½ cup chopped celery
- ½ cup chopped green pepper
- 1 clove minced garlic
- ½ to 1 teaspoon paprika
- 1 to 2 teaspoons dill weed
- 2 tablespoons minced fresh parsley
  —J.K.

Basic Salmon Patties

Another recipe that we just had to include—even though it wasn't submitted—was salmon patties. Canned salmon has long been an economical ingredient, and many Hoosiers grew up knowing that salmon patties would often appear on the dinner table. Today, you will frequently find them as the Friday special at small-town cafes. In fact, fish of some type or another is common on Fridays—perhaps a remnant of the pre–Vatican II Catholic tradition of abstaining from meat.

>   1 **(14.75-ounce) can salmon**
>   1 **egg**
> ½ **cup fine dry bread crumbs**
> ¼ **cup finely chopped onion**
>   2 **tablespoons mayonnaise**
>   **olive oil for frying**

Drain salmon thoroughly, reserving liquid. Place in bowl and flake with fork. Beat together egg and bread crumbs; add onion and mayonnaise, stirring well to combine. Add mixture to salmon, stirring until combined. Shape into four or five patties, adding a bit of reserved liquid if necessary.

In a large nonstick skillet, heat 1 tablespoon olive oil over medium heat. Carefully add patties to skillet and cook, turning once, until browned on each side, adding more oil if needed. Remove from skillet and drain on paper towels. Serve immediately. Serves 4.

Cook's note: Control oil droplets from going everywhere by using a spatter cover. And to lessen the fish smell, simmer a quartered lemon in water on the stove for a while after cooking, or set out a bowl of vinegar afterward. These are old solutions to the problem.

Cabbage Casserole

NEL'S CAFE, OSSIAN
Pieternella "Nel" Geurs

Nel tried this easy, yet flavorful casserole at a friend's house years ago and loved it. "I have made it for my customers to try and so far the response has been good," she says. It's like stuffed cabbage without the work.

> 2 **pounds ground beef**
> 1 **medium onion, chopped**
>   **salt and pepper**
> 1 **medium head cabbage, shredded**
> 1 **can tomato soup**
> ¼ **cup water**

Cook ground beef with chopped onion; drain. Season to taste with salt and pepper.

In a 9-by-13-inch baking pan, place a layer of shredded cabbage. Top with a layer of ground beef. Repeat, ending with ground beef.

Mix tomato soup and water and pour over the top of casserole. Cover and bake at 400 degrees for 1 hour. Serves 6.

Sausage and Sauerkraut

VELMA'S DINER, SHOALS
Debbie Montgomery

Both sausage and sauerkraut are evidence of Indiana's German heritage. This dish is served on Mondays at Velma's Diner as an alternative to ham and beans. The flavorful recipe is a breeze to prepare and makes an easy weeknight supper. For a traditional taste, choose sauerkraut with caraway and use kielbasa.

> 1 **(16-ounce) jar sauerkraut**
>   **scant ¼ cup sugar**
> 1 **pound smoked sausage**

Place sauerkraut with juice in a deep skillet; stir in sugar. Add smoked sausage, cut into pieces, if desired. Cook, stirring occasionally, over low heat until sausage is heated through. Serves 4.

Sausage and Cabbage

BOBBIE JO'S DINER, EDINBURGH
Bobbie Jo Hart

Cook Bertha Burton has been in the restaurant business for more than fifty years. As the owner of Bertha's Place in downtown Edinburgh, she became something of a local institution. Not long after she sold her cafe and retired, she was back cooking at Bobbie Jo's Diner. This recipe for sausage and cabbage is an old favorite carried over from Bertha's Place.

> $\frac{1}{2}$ **cup butter**
> 3 **large onions, sliced thin**
> 1 **garlic clove, minced**
> 1 **small head cabbage, cored and chopped**
> 1 **pound smoked sausage**
> 2 **cups thick-style egg noodles**

In a heavy pot or dutch oven, melt butter. Add sliced onions and cook over low heat, stirring occasionally, until onions are soft and beginning to brown; add garlic.

Add cabbage, stirring into onions, and continue to cook over low heat. Cut smoked sausage into $\frac{1}{2}$-inch slices; cut slices in half. Add to onions and cabbage and simmer over low heat.

Cook noodles according to package directions; drain and add other ingredients, stirring well to combine. Simmer until cabbage is tender. Serves 4 to 6.

Baked Spaghetti

JANET'S KITCHEN, RENSSELAER
Janet and Ken Delaney

Janet found this recipe in a copy of *Taste of Home* magazine, and it immediately drew rave reviews from the regular crowd at her namesake cafe, where a sign above the coffee table reads: "This table reserved for farmers, fishermen, golfers, and other liars."

"When I make this, I double or triple the amount," she says. "There is none left at the end of the day. Every time I make this dish, I get requests for the recipe." We're not lying when we say we're glad she's shared it.

- 1 **cup chopped onions**
- 1 **cup chopped green pepper**
- 1 **tablespoon butter or margarine**
- 1 **(28-ounce) can tomatoes with liquid, cut up**
- 1 **(4-ounce) can mushroom stems and pieces, drained**
- 1 **(2¼-ounce) can sliced ripe olives, drained**
- 2 **teaspoons dried oregano**
- 1 **pound ground beef, browned and drained**
- 12 **ounces spaghetti, cooked and drained**
- 2 **cups shredded cheddar cheese**
- 1 **can condensed cream of mushroom soup**
- ¼ **cup water**
- ¼ **cup grated parmesan cheese**

In a large skillet sauté onions and green pepper in butter until tender. Add tomatoes, mushrooms, olives, and oregano. Add cooked ground beef. Simmer, uncovered, for 10 minutes.

Place half of the spaghetti in a greased 9-by-13-inch baking dish. Top with half of the vegetable-meat mixture. Sprinkle with 1 cup cheddar cheese. Repeat layers.

Mix the soup and water until smooth; pour over casserole. Sprinkle with parmesan cheese. Bake uncovered at 350 degrees for 30 to 35 minutes or until heated through. Serves 12.

Yesiga We't
(Mild Beef or Lamb Stew)

DANIEL'S LIGONIER CAFE, LIGONIER
Daniel Alemu

Immigrants new to this country often find success in the restaurant business, adding ethnic specialties to cafe menus and introducing diners to new flavors that happily coexist with traditional ones. This Ethiopian recipe is a fragrant and flavorful twist on a traditional beef or lamb stew.

   1 **pound cubed beef or lamb for stew**
   1 **cup purified spiced butter (see page 50)**
   4 **cups chopped yellow onion**
   ½ **teaspoon turmeric**
   ½ **teaspoon ground ginger**
   1 **teaspoon minced garlic**
      salt to taste

Remove any fat from meat. Cook meat in 2 quarts boiling water for 3 minutes. Remove the meat and set aside.

In a medium pot, melt spiced butter; add onion, and cook over low heat until onion turns light brown, about 5 to 10 minutes. Add turmeric, ginger, and garlic, stirring occasionally. Continue to cook until mixture boils; lower heat and simmer 3 to 5 more minutes. Add meat and simmer, covered, until meat is tender, about 45 minutes. Serves 4.

DANIEL'S LIGONIER CAFE

Sarah at the Noble County Convention and Visitors Bureau tipped me off to Daniel's Ligonier Cafe. "It's a great place, and they have Ethiopian or some kind of ethnic food once a week."

Huh? A cafe in Indiana's marshmallow capital serving Ethiopian food? Either Sarah had made a mistake or I didn't hear her correctly over the phone. Some weeks later, I happened to be passing through Ligonier after every downtown door was locked. I was so curious about Daniel's that I pulled to the curb and got out. With my hands cupped around my face, I peered into the darkened cafe.

"Are you looking for Daniel?" a voice called out from across the street.

I turned to see a man silhouetted in a lit doorway. "No," I replied evasively, stammering something about Ethiopian food.

"Oh, yeah, that's right," the silhouette tells me. "Every Friday night. You've got to come between five and eight. Daniel's Ethiopian."

Daniel came to America in 1982. He lived in New York before moving on to Clarion University in Clarion, Pennsylvania, where he received an undergraduate degree in computer science. He returned home to New York confident he'd soon be hired for the perfect full-time position, but freelance work was the only thing that came his way. Family members in Fort Wayne encouraged him to try the Hoosier state, and when his computer science degree again failed to produce a job, he began to consider other options. "I'd always liked to cook," he says, "so I began looking for a restaurant and found this one." After spending about six months working with the previous owners, he welcomed his first customers in July 1994.

"My first day was terrifying," he remembers. "I couldn't sleep all night. I finally fell asleep at four o'clock and woke up late. The previous owners are amazed I'm still here! A *lot* of people are amazed I'm still here."

Daniel describes his menu as "mostly Hoosier food made from scratch." Every day he prepares four or five daily specials, like meat loaf, hamburger steak, burgers, and soup and sandwich combinations to feed his friends in Ligonier. But after 5 p.m. on Fridays, the locals who are not culturally curious are rarely to be found. Daniel estimates that 99 percent of the people on hand for Ethiopian fare come from out of town, with the Goshen College "contingent" being his best customers. Many of the students get their first taste of native food—and their first try at the traditional way of eating it—at Daniel's before heading to Ethiopia for overseas study or Mennonite mission work.

My companion and I watch the students intently for tips on how best to approach the platters of unusual food that Daniel carries out to us. He is used to coaching new recruits and spends a few minutes putting us through our warm ups before letting us master the plays.

"We don't use knives and forks in Ethiopia," Daniel explains. Instead, he shows us how to pinch a piece of injera, a fermented flat bread made from teff (an Ethiopian cereal grain that is ground into flour), between our thumb and fingers and use it to carry food from our plates to our lips. In the absence of American table utensils, injera is a culturally consistent (and at first a bit awkward) way of enjoying Daniel's traditional Ethiopian dinner selections.

We didn't want to miss out on anything, so we ordered the combination platter that included a spicy beef dish known as wot, a chicken leg paired with a hard-boiled egg ("chicken and egg go together traditionally

in Ethiopia"), pink lentils, and a vegetable stew made with potatoes, carrots, green beans, and snap peas. The meal includes hot injera and cottage cheese, used to clear off the lingering burn of onions, red peppers, and other spices used in both the wot and lentils.

"Ethiopia is the only country in the world making food like this," Daniel says. "No one else uses teff. When I came to America in 1982, there was one old woman operating an Ethiopian restaurant in Washington, D.C. She used to make injera by substituting flour for the teff and using lemon juice to give it the sour taste. . . . Chinese food, Mexican food, you can find it everywhere. It's become Americanized, I think. Ethiopia is the only country in the world making food like this. Ethiopian food is unique."—J.S., adapted from *Cafe Indiana*

Yeteneter Qibe (Purified Spice Butter)

DANIEL'S LIGONIER CAFE, LIGONIER
Daniel Alemu

Purified, or clarified, butter enhanced with spices is an essential component of many Ethiopian dishes. Thankfully, it is quite easy to make. Butter is slowly heated until the fat and milk solids and lactose separate, then strained to leave a rich, clear oil. Qibe, or ghee, can be stored in the refrigerator or freezer until needed.

> **3 pounds butter**
> ¼ **cup chopped fresh ginger**
> ¼ **cup chopped garlic**
> ¼ **teaspoon ground cumin**
> ¼ **teaspoon basil**
> ¼ **teaspoon cardamom seeds**
> ¼ **teaspoon oregano**
> ¼ **teaspoon turmeric**

In a 4-quart pot, melt butter over low heat, stirring occasionally. When completely melted, add remaining ingredients and simmer, stirring gently, until foam subsides. Remove from heat and let stand 10 minutes. Strain into a lidded container, cool, and store, covered, in a cool place. Makes 3 pounds.

Yesiga We't
(Hot Beef or Lamb Stew)

DANIEL'S LIGONIER CAFE, LIGONIER
Daniel Alemu

This spicy stew is a variation on Daniel's mild version and is punched up considerably with the addition of generous amounts of paprika and chili powder. Try it with the full amounts for an authentically spicy taste, or cut them down for a less potent version.

    1 cup purified butter (see page 50)
    4 cups chopped yellow onion
    ½ cup tomato paste
    ½ teaspoon ground ginger
    1 teaspoon garlic powder
    ½ cup paprika
    ¼ cup chili powder
    2 cups water, divided
    1 pound cubed stew beef or lamb
      salt to taste

In a medium pot, melt butter; add onion and continue to cook over low heat until onion turns light brown (5 to 10 minutes). Add tomato paste, ginger, garlic powder, paprika, and chili powder, stirring well with each addition to make sure ingredients are well mixed. Bring to a simmer and add 1 cup water. Continue to simmer until onion is cooked. Add remaining cup water and the meat. Cover and simmer until meat is cooked, about 45 minutes, adding additional water if necessary. Serves 4.

Doro We't (Chicken Stew)

DANIEL'S LIGONIER CAFE, LIGONIER
Daniel Alemu

Chicken and eggs are a typical combo in Ethiopian cooking, and this spicy stew features both in what is a classic dish. Although this stew is typically quite spicy, feel free to adjust the amounts of paprika and chili powder; cutting them in half will still yield a robust dish.

> 1 **cup purified spice butter (see page 50)**
> 4 **cups chopped yellow onion**
> ½ **cup tomato paste**
> ½ **teaspoon ground ginger**
> 1 **teaspoon garlic powder**
> ½ **cup paprika**
> ¼ **cup chili powder**
> 2 **cups water, divided**
> 6 **chicken drumsticks**
> 6 **hard-cooked eggs**
> **salt to taste**

In a medium pot, melt butter; add onion and continue to cook over low heat until onion turns light brown (5 to 10 minutes). Add tomato paste, ginger, garlic powder, paprika, and chili powder, stirring well after each addition to make sure ingredients are completely mixed. Bring to a simmer and add 1 cup water. Continue to simmer until onion is cooked. Remove the skin and fat from chicken; rinse well. Add remaining cup of water, the eggs, and chicken. Cover and simmer until chicken is cooked, about 30 to 40 minutes, adding additional water if necessary. Serves 4.

Mild Split Pea or Lentil Sauce

DANIEL'S LIGONIER CAFE, LIGONIER
Daniel Alemu

Like Daniel's chicken and beef stews, this dish—essentially a split pea or lentil stew—is meant to be served with thin, pliable injera bread, which diners use to pick up a bite. But it's just as good eaten with a fork. Feel free to cut back on the jalapeno, if desired.

> ¼ **cup corn oil**
> 2 **cups chopped yellow onion**
> 1 **tablespoon minced fresh ginger**
> 1½ **tablespoons crushed garlic**
> 4 **cups water**
> ¼ **teaspoon turmeric**
> 2 **cups split peas or yellow lentils**
> 2 **jalapeño peppers**
> **salt to taste**

In a medium pot, heat oil and cook onions on low heat until lightly brown. Add ginger and garlic and simmer 1 minute. Add water and turmeric; bring to boil, stirring occasionally.

Rinse peas or lentils and add to pot. Return mixture to a boil, then lower heat and simmer about 30 minutes or until peas or lentils are nearly tender, stirring occasionally. Cut ends from jalapeño and, wearing rubber gloves, carefully remove seeds and white membranes; cut each jalapeno lengthwise into 4 strips and add to sauce. Continue to simmer for about another 30 minutes, adding additional water if necessary. Season with salt to taste. Serves 4.

THREE

~ ~ ~

Soups and Sandwiches

Chili #1

CHAMBERS SMORGASBORD, SPENCER
Barbara Chambers and Jim Chambers

Barbara created this mild yet flavorful chili, adjusting a basic chili recipe "until it suited me," she says, noting that her son, Jim, added the cayenne pepper and the cumin. It is quite mild as chili goes; for a bolder version, substitute V-8 juice for the water and increase the amount of chili powder.

2½ pounds ground beef
1 medium onion, diced
1 (46-ounce) can tomato juice
3 quarts water
3 (15-ounce) cans kidney beans
½ cup sugar
⅓ cup chili powder
1½ teaspoons cumin
dash cayenne pepper
1 tablespoon salt
1½ teaspoons pepper
1 (16-ounce) box elbow macaroni

Brown ground beef with onion; drain. In a large pot, combine meat mixture with tomato juice, water, beans, sugar, and spices. Bring to a boil; reduce heat and simmer 1 hour.

Cook macaroni in rapidly boiling salted water just until tender; drain. Add to chili, stirring well to combine. Cook over low heat, stirring occasionally, an additional 10 minutes. Serves 6.

Chili #2

CAFE MAX, CULVER
Susie Mahler

This version of chili, made with plenty of beans, pepperoncini, and a generous amount of chili powder, offers a well-seasoned take on the cafe classic. You can offer such toppings as sour cream or shredded cheddar, but don't forget the saltines—although many folks like oyster crackers with chili, just like those in the little packages served at the cafe.

- 1½ pounds ground beef
- 1 cup chopped onion
- chopped pepperoncini, to taste
- ¼ cup chili powder
- 2 teaspoons cumin
- ½ teaspoon cayenne pepper
- 1 tablespoon sugar
- ½ teaspoon salt
- 3 (30.5-ounce) cans chili beans with liquid
- 2 teaspoons beef base
- 1 (46-ounce) can tomato juice

In a heavy saucepan or dutch oven, brown ground beef with onion and pepperoncini; drain. Return beef mixture to pan and add chili powder, cumin, cayenne, sugar, and salt. Add chili beans and beef base and simmer for 15 minutes. Add tomato juice and simmer for 30 more minutes. Serves 6.

Cook's note: Look for jars of pepperoncini with the pickles and relishes in most supermarkets.

Hoosier Chili With

I grew up in a chili-without-noodles family, where elbow macaroni was reserved for macaroni salad and my mom's tomato and hamburger goulash (her contribution to every community supper we ever attended), and spaghetti noodles never made an appearance outside of spaghetti itself. My husband, on the other hand, grew up with chili-with-noodles folks who "stretched the pot" by adding elbow macaroni that swelled to soft, curly tubes. Needless to say, my husband, Mark, and I faced serious ideological and experiential differences when we married: would ours be a chili-with or a chili-without union? Since I do all of the cooking, Mark has graciously ceded to the "without" side of the coin, and our son, Pete, of course, has followed suit.

In *Chili Nation*, Jane and Michael Stern claim a Tex-Mex heritage for chili, placing its birthplace in and around San Antonio. With its ground beef, kidney beans, and tomato sauce—not to mention its noodles—midwestern chili is as far from the sirloin and pepper-packed Texas red as one can get. If chili is, as the Sterns believe, "this country's one truly shared national food," then the kettle in which it's cooked is the nation's true melting pot.

As unlikely as it seems, we midwesterners may well have Greek, Macedonian, and other European immigrants to thank for the antecedents to our favorite "chili with." In Cincinnati, Macedonian brothers from the lower Manhattan area of New York City concocted a chili sauce with traditional spices like cardamom, coriander, cinnamon, cloves, and cumin, and then stirred in finely ground beef. First used to top wieners—the Coney Island–style hot dog—it evolved into the famous two-, three- four-, and five-way chili plates, all of which include a base layer of spaghetti noodles layered with chili sauce. Your choice of kidney beans, chopped raw onions, and orange cheddar cheese make up the rest of the "ways." Cincinnati-style chili restaurants familiar to Hoosiers include Skyline Chili, which has been in the Indianapolis area for many years; a few are also found in the southeast part of the state, along with Gold Star and Empress outlets.

While Cincinnati-style chili may be the Midwest's contribution to our Chili Nation, plain old Hoosier chili with noodles is far more likely to be the chili in every Colts fan's pot. We make it by simmering browned ground beef and kidney beans in a tomatoey liquid—tomato juice, V-8 juice, even condensed tomato soup—spiced just oh-so-slightly with chili powder and maybe a touch of cumin, and "stretched" with elbow macaroni or broken spaghetti. Hoosiers are not really layerers, unless, that is, you consider our habit of crushing saltines or corn bread over the top of a bowl and stirring in the crumbs to make a kind of chili mush. A Hoosier Two-Way, maybe?—J.S., adapted from *Cafe Wisconsin Cookbook*

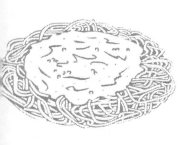

Beef and Cabbage Soup

Cafe Max, Culver
Susie Mahler

This hearty beef and cabbage soup developed by Cafe Max's ace of soups, Ron Bowers, is an easy one-pot meal that's perfect for a chilly evening. While it's full of vegetables as is, this soup offers plenty of room for improvisation. It's great with an addition of canned diced tomatoes and chopped fresh zucchini.

- 1 **pound stew beef, cut into bite-size pieces**
- 2 **tablespoons vegetable oil**
- 1 **onion, chopped**
- 1 **teaspoon garlic powder**
- 1½ **teaspoons dry mustard**
- 1 **head cabbage, shredded**
- 1 **cup green pepper, chopped**
- 1 **cup beef base**
- 2 **quarts water**
- 5 **potatoes, peeled and diced**
- 2 **cups frozen or canned corn**

In a heavy saucepan or dutch oven, brown stew beef in hot oil; add onions and sauté until they begin to soften. Stir in garlic powder and dry mustard. Add cabbage and green pepper. Dissolve beef base in water; add to pan, stirring well. Bring to a boil; reduce heat and simmer for about 45 minutes. Add potatoes; increase heat and cook until potatoes are tender. Add corn and simmer until heated through. Serves 6.

Stuffed Pepper Soup

NEL'S CAFE, OSSIAN
Pieternella "Nel" Geurs

A good friend gave Nel this recipe, which she then tried out at the cafe. "It was liked by all," says Nel. "I even handed out the recipe." The tasty soup is easy to liven up with the addition of Italian seasoning, garlic powder, and other spices. For more kick, use seasoned diced tomatoes, such as Ro-tel brand.

- 1 pound ground beef
- 1 quart water
- 1 (14.5-ounce) can diced tomatoes
- 1 (14.5-ounce) can tomato sauce
- ½ cup cooked rice
- 1 cup chopped bell pepper
- 1 beef bouillon cube
- 1 tablespoon, packed, brown sugar
- 1 teaspoon salt
- ½ teaspoon pepper

In a large saucepan or dutch oven, brown ground beef; drain. Return beef to saucepan and add remaining ingredients; bring to a boil. Reduce heat, cover, and simmer for 30 to 40 minutes. Serves 8.

Chicken Soup

JULIE'S TELL STREET CAFE, TELL CITY
Julie Fischer

Julie uses leftover baked or fried chicken for this basic, yet comforting soup, one that is on the menu every day. "It makes you feel better when you're not feeling good," says Julie. "I swear by that."

- 2 quarts water
- 1 tablespoon chicken base, or more to taste
- 1 pound baby carrots, sliced
- 1 package peppered gravy mix
- 1 ½ cups wide egg noodles

2 cups diced cooked chicken
1 (12-ounce) bag frozen peas

Heat water in a large pot or dutch oven over medium-high heat; stir in chicken base. Add carrots, bring to a boil, and cook just until carrots are tender.

Meanwhile, combine gravy mix with half the amount of water called for on package. Stir into soup. Return soup to a boil and add noodles.

When noodles are nearly done, add cooked chicken along with peas. Simmer until chicken and peas are heated through. Serves 6 to 8.

Chicken Florentine Soup

CORNER CAFE, WAKARUSA
Candy and Alan Krull

"I don't remember where I got the recipe. Isn't that funny? I guess I thought I'd never forget," Candy's mom, Marsha Thomas, says of this tasty version of chicken soup. Many customers order a cup of it along with the daily special, she says, noting that one Nappanee shop owner orders two gallons of it every Christmas.

4 tablespoons butter
1 cup flour
1½ quarts chicken stock
2 cups diced cooked chicken
¼ cup pimentos (optional)
1 small (6-ounce) bag baby spinach leaves
1 cup half-and-half
salt and pepper

In a heavy saucepan or dutch oven, melt butter; add flour. Cook, stirring, 2 minutes. Add chicken stock, whisking until smooth. Add chicken and pimento, if using. Bring to a boil.

Reduce heat and add spinach and half-and-half, stirring to combine. Season to taste with salt and pepper. Serves 4 to 6.

Cook's note: For a lighter, broth-based soup, omit the half-and-half.

Tortellini Soup

MARTY'S BLUEBIRD CAFE, LAKETON
Martha "Marty" and Bart Huffman

Loaded with vegetables and flavored with basil, oregano, and red wine, Tortellini Soup is a hearty soup, appealing in warm weather and cold. Add some crusty bread and make a meal of it.

    1   pound hot bulk sausage
    1   cup chopped onion
    2   large cloves garlic, chopped
    6   cups beef stock
    1   (14.5-ounce) can diced tomatoes
    1   (8-ounce) can tomato sauce
    1   medium zucchini, sliced
    2   large carrots, sliced
    2   ribs celery, sliced
  1/2   cup dry red wine
    1   teaspoon dried basil
    2   teaspoons oregano
    1   (8-ounce) package cheese tortellini
        freshly grated parmesan (optional)

In a heavy skillet, brown sausage; drain. Add onion and garlic and sauté 5 minutes. In a large soup pot, combine sausage mixture with remaining ingredients except tortellini and parmesan. Simmer until vegetables are tender. Add tortellini; cook until tender. Serve topped with parmesan, if desired. Serves 6 to 8.

Ham and Beans

VELMA'S DINER, SHOALS
Debbie Montgomery

Ham and beans is served on Monday at Velma's Diner along with fried potatoes and corn bread. Debbie typically uses pinto beans, but feel free to use the Great Northern variety if you like. Crumble in a piece of corn bread (recipes on pages 94 and 95) for an authentic taste.

  1 **(16-ounce) package pinto beans**
  2 **quarts water**
  1 **ham hock**
  1 **cup chopped ham**
  ¼ **cup chopped onion**
  1 **tablespoon butter**
     salt and pepper

Soak beans for 8 hours or overnight. Drain, rinse, and pick over, discarding shriveled beans. Place beans in a large, heavy pot and add 2 quarts water and ham hock. Bring to a boil and simmer over medium heat for about an hour, adding water if necessary, until beans are tender. Add chopped ham and onion; simmer until onions are tender. Add butter, stirring to melt. Season to taste with salt and pepper. Serves 4.

WASHDAY HAM AND BEANS

A steaming bowl of soft-cooked beans and chunks of ham served with a side of corn bread and crispy fried potatoes is a Hoosier staple both at home and out and about. Fans of ham and beans should check out the Cataract Bean Dinner and Flea Market held the first weekend in October by the Cataract volunteer fire department. Four or five giant tripods are set up in front of the fire station—its rigs pulled out and doors thrown open to become a makeshift community dining room—and Great Northern beans are cooked low and slow in heavy kettles over an open fire. Delish!

Part of the Hoosier state's Appalachian culinary heritage, ham and beans is a predictable Monday special at most cafes, although the dish is so popular you'll often find it later in the week as well. "Mondays is ham and beans because it was traditionally washday," when a woman's time was consumed by laundry, not cooking, explains Betty Melton, co-owner

with her husband, Sonny, of Sonny's Restaurant in Hartford City. "When we were growing up, Monday was washday. Mother would put on five or six pounds of beans and cook them all day. She'd make fried potatoes and corn bread, and that would be dinner. She didn't have an electric washer or dryer. She'd hang lines in the utility shed and take them down at the end of the day."

White Great Northern beans are the bean of choice for most cafe owners and cooks, but in southern Indiana you'll be just as likely to find brown pinto beans being used. Pinto beans are a staple of Appalachian cooking and appear in menu selections as varied as chili and pie. When long-simmered with ham, smoked pork, and/or bacon, they become soup beans, a dish so popular and ingrained that Mark F. Sohn, in his book *Appalachian Home Cooking*, places it on "the list of famous Southern soups and stews."

At Velma's Diner in Shoals, owner Debbie Montgomery uses pinto beans mostly but will occasionally substitute Great Northerns. "My customers prefer dark," she says. Steve Deckard, publisher of the *Shoals News*, sticks his head in the rear kitchen door every Monday morning and asks, "What color are they today?" If the answer is white, he wrinkles up his nose. —J.S.

BLT Soup

CORNER CAFE, WAKARUSA
Candy and Alan Krull

Customers were hesitant to try this soup at first because the hot lettuce didn't sound appealing, explains Marsha Thomas, who passed the Corner Cafe on to her daughter, Candy, yet retained her place in the kitchen. So she began offering small samples of the flavorful soup. "Everyone who tried it liked it," she says. It's even better with a bit of Dijon-style mustard stirred in at the last minute.

- ½ pound bacon, chopped
- ½ cup diced onions
- ½ cup flour
- 1½ quarts chicken stock
- 2 medium tomatoes, diced (or a 14.5-ounce can diced tomatoes)
- ½ head lettuce, chopped
- 1 cup half-and-half

$\frac{1}{2}$ teaspoon salt
$\frac{1}{8}$ teaspoon pepper

In a heavy saucepan or dutch oven, brown bacon; add onions, cooking until tender. Add flour and cook, stirring, 2 minutes. Add chicken stock and mix well. Add tomatoes and simmer 10 minutes. Add lettuce, half-and-half, and salt and pepper; simmer 10 minutes and serve. Serves 4 to 6.

Cook's note: For a bit more zest, add 2 teaspoons of Dijon-style mustard.

Coney Dog

BABY BOOMERS CAFE, HAMILTON
Penny Hawkins

Is it a coney dog or a chili dog? The absence of beans might place this Baby Boomers Cafe version of the drive-in classic in the coney category, but some might say the thick sauce makes it a chili dog. It's nothing like the dogs served at Fort Wayne's Famous Coney Island, for example, but no matter—it's still mighty good, even better topped with cheese, which, of course, makes it a cheesy dog.

1$\frac{1}{4}$ pounds ground beef
2$\frac{1}{2}$ cups water
  $\frac{1}{3}$ cup barbecue sauce
    heaping $\frac{1}{2}$ teaspoon dried basil
  $\frac{1}{2}$ teaspoon cayenne pepper
  1 tablespoon plus 1 scant teaspoon granulated garlic
  $\frac{1}{4}$ cup chili powder
  6 tablespoons cumin
  6 hot dogs and buns

In a large, heavy skillet, cook ground beef; drain. Return to skillet. Add remaining ingredients. Cook over medium heat until mixture simmers. Cook for approximately 1 hour, stirring to keep mixture from sticking.

Cook hot dogs, place in buns, and top with sauce. Garnish with chopped onions, shredded cheese, and other condiments, as desired. Serves 4 to 6.

Fried ~~Bologna~~ Baloney

A tradition in many Hoosier families, fried bologna on classic squishy white bread is a sandwich packed with fond lunchtime and after-school memories. The seasoned luncheon meat is the bastard child of a specialty sausage produced in Bologna, Italy, but here in the States it's lost any semblance of pretentiousness. Wholesomely egalitarian, it's baloney all the way—except when we affectionately dub it "hillbilly hamburger," "Hoosier steak," and "redneck ribeye." And that sandwich? Some folks insist if it's fried baloney, it's got to be "sammich."

"I make fried baloney with a side of sweet pickles . . . I been hillbilly since way back when," sings country performer Neal McCoy in "Rednecktified." NASCAR driver Elliott Sadler chows down back-home baloney burgers made with plenty of butter-grilled onions, a top draw at the concession stands at South Boston Speedway in Virginia. Even Hardee's has joined what Slashfood blogger Hanna Raskin calls a "minor bologna renaissance" with its fried baloney, egg, and cheese breakfast biscuit, a request of some southern franchisees.

On Wonder Bread, on a bun, or on a biscuit—how do you like your fried baloney sammich? Eat it cold or grilled and slathered with real mayonnaise, a smear of plain yellow mustard, or Open Pit. Add a slice of processed American cheese or Velveeta. Add a fried egg—or not. Spread pickle relish between the slices of bread or off to the side, alternating a bite of sandwich and a forkful of relish. Alas, no baloney? Substitute hot dogs sliced lengthwise, as is popular at the Dinner Bell in Salem. At Windell's Cafe in Dale and Harold's Restaurant in Poseyville, you'll find garlicky German-style baloney served cold or fried.

At the end of a long weekend, a familiar Hoosier quick Sunday supper is fried baloney gravy. Remove the fried slices from the pan, dice them into bits and set aside. Make a milk-based gravy using the oily pan drippings, then stir in the diced baloney. Serve over toast or biscuits. —J.S.

Fried Bologna Sandwich

Jackie's Family Restaurant, Gas City
Jackie and Merle Ingle

"Fried bologna was a must for my husband," says Jackie. "I thought it was a silly idea but time proved me wrong. We have businessmen order it because they haven't had it since they were a kid or ever seen it on a menu." Native Hoosier David Letterman of late-night TV fame

is a well-known fan of fried bologna sandwiches. Jackie buys her bologna from a supermarket deli case.

> 1 **pound beef bologna (such as Eckrich), cut in**
> **¼-inch-thick slices**
> 1 **tablespoon cooking oil or as needed**
> 4 **hamburger buns**

Cut four slits into each slice of bologna along outside edges so it doesn't cup when heated. Heat oil in nonstick skillet and cook bologna slices for a minute or two on each side, until heated through and beginning to brown.

Toast hamburger buns and serve bologna on buns. Top with condiments and/or sliced American cheese, if desired. Serves 4.

Theatre Cafe Double Feature

Wolcott Theatre Cafe, Wolcott
Ann Cain

Definitely not for the light eater, the Theatre Cafe Double Feature was introduced by a waitress who remembered it from a restaurant in her Illinois hometown. "People sauce it up with ketchup, mustard, hot sauce, Worcestershire," says Ann. "I kind of thought, well! But they love it." It's hard to deny the appeal of a burger and fries topped with cheese sauce.

> 1 **pound frozen french fries**
> 1 **(15-ounce) jar cheese sauce (such as Cheez Whiz**
> **or Velveeta brand)**
> 4 **(¼-pound) burger patties**
> 2 **onions, sliced**
> **butter**
> 4 **slices Texas toast**

Prepare fries according to package directions. Warm the cheese sauce in microwave. On a griddle or in a large skillet (working in batches if necessary) grill burger patties for 5 minutes per side. Sauté onions on grill alongside. Lightly butter and grill the Texas toast.

To assemble, place a piece of toast on each plate; top each with a burger. Evenly distribute onions and then fries atop burgers. Drizzle hot cheese over everything; garnish, if desired, with sliced jalapenos, diced tomatoes, or chopped pepper. Serve with hot sauce on the side. Serves 4.

IF I ONLY HAD A BRAIN

The demise of what may be Indiana's quirkiest cafe food has come and gone with barely a notice, except, perhaps, by the handful of women at Julie Fischer's Tell City cafe for whom eating a fried brain sandwich was a weekly ritual. The odd delicacy is found in the Hoosier state primarily near Evansville, passed down by German immigrants who settled in the Ohio River valley.

Until the fear of mad cow disease led the USDA to ban the sale of brains from cattle older than thirty months, cow brains were the stuff of choice. Now you'll have to settle for pig brains—what most connoisseurs feel is an inferior substitute because it is harder to cook, falls apart easily, and doesn't have as much flavor.

"I hate to burst your bubble, but I don't have them anymore," Julie informed me when I asked for a recipe for fried brain sandwich. "I stopped because I just couldn't stand making them."

Her revulsion was shared by Donna Green, owner of DJ's Main Street Cafe in Rockport—now closed—where they had been a longstanding menu item. "Making them makes me sick, but I do it," she had told me, pinching her nose with her thumb and forefinger and wrinkling up her brow. "I stand there fixing them and ask anyone watching if they want to try one. If they don't like them, they won't eat them. I don't get any new people giving them a try."

Where Julie worked with fresh brains, Donna preferred frozen because they are precleaned, meaning she didn't have to separate the brains from the surrounding membrane. "I can't handle fresh brains," she told me. Donna would knead the brains together with a batter of eggs, flour, baking powder, and salt and pepper, shape them into patties, and then fry them on the grill until they held together in a reasonably solid form. Into the freezer they went, waiting for the day someone walked through the door with a hankering for a fried brain sandwich.

Years back, it was common to find fried brains served at local fairs and festivals, in taverns, and on the breakfast tables of folks of German heritage. You'll still find them at the West Side Nut Club Fall Festival in Evansville, but they're mostly tavern food nowadays. You can't go wrong launching your quest at the Hilltop Inn in Evansville, named "Manliest Restaurant in America" in 2009 by Asylum.com. No doubt we must pause and acknowledge the fried brain sandwich's part in this triumph. "There's definitely something about mashing up something's brain, frying it in a pan and dropping it on a bun that's guaranteed to put hair on your chest.

This is a proud day for the brain eaters throughout our fifty states and around the world," extolled Asylum editor-in-chief Neil Gladstone. —J.S.

Fried Brain Sandwich

JULIE'S TELL STREET CAFE, TELL CITY
Julie Fischer

Julie served fried brain sandwiches for a long time, although she never enjoyed making them. "The same people tended to order these," says Julie, who has taken them off the menu. "We used to have a group of women who came in. They so looked forward to their brain sandwiches." Pork brains can sometimes be found in ethnic markets, or ask at your local butcher shop.

1 **pound frozen pork brains**
2 **eggs**
3 **tablespoons flour**
$\frac{1}{2}$ **teaspoon salt**
$\frac{1}{2}$ **teaspoon pepper**
 oil for frying
4 **hamburger buns**

Thaw brains; place in medium bowl. Working under cold running water, rinse brains, removing any membranes, carefully handling brains and tearing them as little as possible. Drain and set aside.

In a separate bowl, stir together eggs and flour; add salt and pepper. Fold in brains, stirring gently.

In a nonstick skillet or on a griddle, heat oil. Using a soup ladle, scoop out about a quarter of mixture and pour into skillet or griddle. Cook over medium heat for several minutes per side or until browned. Serve on buns and top with desired condiments. Serves 4.

Breaded Pork Tenderloin #1 🟦

NEWBERRY CAFE, NEWBERRY
Lanny and Lois Pickett

Ask any Hoosier foodie. There's no single way to make a great BPT. You'll be told as many "recipes" as there are taverns, drive-ins, bowling alleys, cafes, and so on and so on where great ones are served. We like this memorable meaty 'loin—it is not pounded and minimally flattened—prepared fresh and by hand every day at the Newberry Cafe, a dream of a diner in a barely there town on Indiana 57 in Greene County.

> **soybean oil**
> 2 **cups flour**
> 2 **cups Marion-Kay Tenderloin Breading**
> 2 **eggs**
> 4 **cups milk**
> 1 to 1½ **pounds boneless pork tenderloin**
> **hamburger buns**

Pour about 3 inches of oil into a frying pan and heat to 350 degrees.

Put flour into a shallow pan and set aside. Put Marion-Kay Tenderloin Breading in a second pan. Beat eggs and milk in a wide bowl and set aside.

Slice the tenderloin as thick or thin as you like, and then butterfly each piece. Using a hand-held Jaccard meat tenderizer with retractable blades, or a very sharp-tined fork, pierce a slice of tenderloin three times on one side, then flip it and pierce three times on the other side.

Dip a slice of tenderloin in the milk mixture, then place it in the flour and push gently so that flour on the underside adheres. Turn the tenderloin over and do the same. Then, repeat the egg and milk bath and dredging, but this time in the breading.

Slide the tenderloin into the hot oil; it should be completely submerged. Cook for 3 to 4 minutes. Cut into the thickest part of the tenderloin to check doneness. Serve hot on a bun with desired condiments and dressings. Serves 4.

Cook's note: Marion-Kay Tenderloin Breading is manufactured by Marion-Kay Spices. You can buy it at the factory outlet store in Brownstown, online at www.marionkay.com, or at specialty stores throughout Indiana—including the Odon Locker. See sidebar.

HEART OF THE MATTER

Unlike Jane and Michael Stern and other breaded pork tenderloin connoisseurs, I am not so bold as to label a particular BPT Indiana's best. This is why, when it came down to selecting representative BPT recipes for this book, I knew I had to include one for the tenderloin made by Lanny and Lois Pickett at the Newberry Cafe. The Picketts' tenderloins are hand cut, butterflied, breaded, and deep-fried delights, thick and juicy, sweet and clean, and unadulterated by overused oil.

The heart of a great BPT is the pork. The Picketts buy fresh, hand-processed tenderloin from the Odon Locker, in Odon, where meat is all meat. "We have a unique way of taking care of things," explains owner Norman Swartzentruber, who bought the locker from his father, Amos, in 1998. "We don't cut any corners. We don't use fillers or additives. We buy fresh product and cut all our own meat."

"Really?" Norman says when I tell him I rate the Newberry tenderloin among the most unforgettable of the hundreds I ate during my Indiana food foray. But really, he is not surprised. "Lanny takes that tenderloin and actually puts that meat on the sandwich. So many people will take a three-ounce piece of meat and add fillers and breading to make it a five-ounce piece. He prepares the meat correctly and uses a good seasoning."

Amos Swartzentruber expanded the Odon Locker by adding a retail store in 1976, when residents still relied on local merchants. Amos's customers were drawn to his fresh, pure meats because they were the same high quality they had known on the family farm. Over the years, many drifted away to distant one-stop stores; others remained steadfastly loyal. Today, the Odon Locker draws customers from a twenty- to thirty-mile radius, according to Norman. "They say our ground beef is the best, but there's no secret to the ground beef. It's just good meat, ground right here. There's very little fat. It's just like the ground beef their grandfather made."

Other signature products at the Odon Locker include award-winning bacon, bratwurst, marinated turkey breast, and steaks. You'll also find the seasoned tenderloin breading Lanny prefers; it's produced by Marion-Kay Spices of Brownstown. —J.S.

Breaded Pork Tenderloin #2 🏴

STORIE'S RESTAURANT, GREENSBURG
Don Storie, Chuck Storie, and Beth Storie-Sanders

With awards and recognition galore, Storie's BPT is, well, storied. Up to five hundred pounds of fresh Canadian back loins are hand trimmed and cut, tenderized, marinated, breaded, pounded, and deep fried every week. The recipe and method came from a Columbus tavern in the 1970s, but both were tweaked by mom Katherine Storie to make them the restaurant's very own. Each tenderloin is made to order, so you can get yours as thick or thin, as small or elephantine as you like. Below is our best attempt at a "recipe" for home kitchens.

> 1 to 1½ pounds fresh Canadian back loin
> 2 eggs
> 4 cups 2-percent milk
>   alternative to "secret recipe breading mix"
>   (see below)
>   vegetable oil
>   hamburger bun

Trim off the side strap of the loin, carefully picking out bone bits, and reserve for pork barbecue (as they do at Storie's). Slice off the ends of the loin and set aside for use as baked pork. Cut the remaining loin into slices 1½ to 2 inches thick or 5 to 6 ounces in weight.

Beat eggs and milk together in large bowl and set aside.

Place "secret recipe breading mix" in a 9-by-13-inch pan. (Since Storie's breading is really a secret, we offer a substitute below.)

Using the flat side of a large meat cleaver, press each slice to flatten slightly, then pound with an aluminum hammer–type tenderizer. At Storie's, the loins are then run through a mechanical cuber, which further flattens them and also tenderizes by piercing and dimpling. If you do not have a cuber, pierce the loin with a meat tenderizer or the sharp tines of a fork.

After tenderizing, place each loin in the egg and milk bath and allow to marinate up to 2 hours.

To cook, heat 3 to 5 inches of vegetable oil in a deep frying pan to 350 degrees. The depth of the oil depends on how thick your BPT will be. (A typical Storie's BPT averages about 9 inches long by 4 to 5 inches wide and is about ⅜ inch thick.)

Remove a loin from the egg and milk bath and place it in the breading mix. Press the loin into the breading mix, flattening and spreading it to the desired thickness and diameter. Flip it over and do the same on the other side. Slide it carefully into the heated oil, taking care that the breading does not fall or rub off.

Cook for about 4 to 5 minutes, or until golden brown.

Serve on a standard size bun, dressed as much or as little as you like. Number of servings varies.

Alternative to "Secret Recipe Breading Mix"

The sturdy breading on Storie's BPT is smooth and flaky, like crust on fried chicken. We're taking a cue from Lanny and Lois Pickett at the Newberry Cafe (see page 70) and hints from Don Storie to suggest the following less-than-secret recipe. Start with this and tweak as you wish—just as Katherine Storie did. The addition of, say, 1 to 1 ½ teaspoons of dry mustard might be a start.

> 1 **cup flour**
> 1 **cup McCormick Golden Dipt Extra Crispy Chicken**
> **Fry Mix**
> **salt and pepper to taste**
> 1½ **teaspoons dry mustard (optional)**

Hoosier Holy Grail

Louisville has the Hot Brown, New Orleans the Po' Boy, the Upper Peninsula of Michigan the Cornish pasty. As sandwiches go, we Hoosiers are darned lucky. We have a whole state, 92 different counties, 36,420 square miles of breaded pork tenderloin potential. Consistently one of the best-selling items on every cafe menu, the pounded orbs of pork have been the holy grail of national, regional, and local foodies since at least 2003, when America's pop culture food gurus, Jane and Michael Stern, penned "Love Me Tenderloin" in the January issue of *Gourmet* magazine. "A pork sandwich so special we stopped wondering, 'What's a Hoosier?'" they wrote.

The original Hoosier BPT is said to have been invented in 1908 when Nick Freinstein of Huntington hawked breaded and fried cutlets between slices of bread from his street cart. Four years later he had saved enough to open Nick's Kitchen, which is still serving customers today. The next BPT innovation came in the 1960s, when Gerald "Whitey" Ware of Greenfield, a local Jim Dandy franchisee, smothered a breaded tenderloin with brown gravy. He trademarked the "wet tenderloin" in 1970. Indiana has one additional claim to fame (although tenderloin aficionados regard it as a bastard sibling): the chopped and shaped Pete's Pride pork fritter, made by Al Pete's Meats in Muncie.

Hands down, we Hoosiers are enraptured by our breaded pork tenderloins, even while sharing them with our neighbors in southern Illinois and the pork-centric states of Missouri and Iowa, two states where the pork producers elevate and promote the sandwich with a Best Tenderloin of the year contest. Is Indiana too humble to follow suit?

Thankfully, there are plenty of folks in pursuit of the Hoosier Holy Grail and willing to share the experience.

First, in 1998, was "In Search of the Famous Hoosier Breaded Pork Tenderloin Sandwich," a short documentary film by Indiana native Jensen Rufe that celebrates the iconic regional dish, its down-on-the-farm roots, its makers and eaters, and the methods and mysteries of making the perfect BPT.

Next came Jane and Michael Stern, America's favorite road foodies, who exposed Indiana's obsession in *Gourmet* magazine. Their ode to deep-fried, pounded pork spotlighted Nick's Kitchen, Mr. Dave's in Manchester, and the now famous and sadly departed Gnaw Bone Food and Fuel in Brown County. Of the three, it was the tenderloin with the quirky place name that tickled the national taste buds. It wasn't long before the cast and crew of the *Today Show* were doing a live broadcast from the Gnaw

Bone gas station–diner. Although the Food and Fuel has since closed, the Gnaw Bone tenderloin can be had at the nearby Salt Creek Golf Retreat. But is it really the same?

Today there are enraptured bloggers. David Stovall, a Speedway native exiled in Minnesota, is the foodie behind www.porktenderloinsandwich .com, "dedicated to the discussion of the breaded deep-fried pork tenderloin sandwich, the pursuit of them, and whatever may come from that pursuit." Check out his site for a handy step-by-step, make-your-own tutorial.

Another blogger is Indianapolis resident and "tenderloin connoisseur" Rick Garrett, author of "All Tenderloins, all the time" at breadedtenderloin .wordpress.com. Allen "don't-forget-the-mustard" Bukoff is behind "Stalking the Wild Breaded Pork Tenderloin in Iowa," "the Web site for breaded pork tenderloin sandwich lovers." Bukoff shares his search at des-loines .blogspot.com. For more endless discussion, check out the Roadfood.com and Chowhound.com forums.

A good place to launch your own pursuit of the state's top-notch BPTs is the Tenderloin Trail recommended by the Indiana Foodways Alliance at indianafoodways.com (see sidebar on pages 116–17). Included is the celebrated sandwich at Storie's Restaurant on the courthouse square in Greensburg.

And of course you can usually get a pork tenderloin grilled instead of breaded and deep fried, admittedly a lighter option. But really, a breaded pork tenderloin is not the place for calorie cutting. —J.S.

FOUR

~ ~ ~

Salads and Dressings

(continued on facing page)

SALAD HEAVEN

On a rainy Friday evening in mid-October, I encountered a forlorn bicyclist in the parking lot at Chambers Smorgasbord in Spencer. He'd ridden all day from Illinois to participate in this weekend's Hilly Hundred bicycle ride, and he was camped out in a tent at McCormick's Creek State Park. The can't-believe-it, never-ending buffet inside Chambers Smorgasbord had restored his energy and his spirits.

Long-distance bicyclists like him demand starchy carbohydrates to fuel them on the road, but peripatetic cafe hunters like me who have overdosed on fried food, mashed potatoes, and pie crave nothing so much as crunchy fresh vegetables. As I lined up at the smorgasbord, my knees quaked. Before me stretched a beautiful bonanza, the mother lode of salad bars. I rejected the skimpy glass salad bowls and reached for

Pea Salad

CHAMBERS SMORGASBORD, SPENCER
Barbara Chambers and Jim Chambers

Barbara found the recipe for this pea salad, a Chambers salad bar staple, in a Mennonite cookbook nearly thirty years ago. "It is very popular with our customers," she says. It's even better with a little extra bacon sprinkled on top.

    2 (10-ounce) packages frozen peas, thawed
    ½ cup diced onion
    ¾ cup shredded cheddar cheese
    ¼ cup crumbled cooked bacon
  1½ cups mayonnaise
    2 tablespoons sugar
    1 teaspoon vinegar

In a large bowl, stir together peas, onion, cheese, and bacon. In a separate bowl, stir together mayonnaise, sugar, and vinegar. Add to pea mixture; mix well. Cover and refrigerate. Serves 4 to 6.

Broccoli and Cauliflower Salad

CHAMBERS SMORGASBORD, SPENCER
Barbara Chambers and Jim Chambers

Variations of this classic recipe, which Barbara found in an old church cookbook, have been passed around for years. When her late husband, Bob, the founder of Spencer's popular restaurant, added the smorgasbord in 1981, the salad found a permanent home. "It's one of our customers' favorite salads," Barbara says.

    1 large bunch broccoli, cut into bite-size pieces
    1 head cauliflower, cut into bite-size pieces
    2 large carrots, thinly sliced
    ⅓ cup diced onion
    8 slices bacon, fried very crisp, crumbled
  1⅓ cups mayonnaise

¹⁄₂ **cup sugar**
2 **tablespoons vinegar**

In a large bowl, combine broccoli, cauliflower, carrots, onion, and bacon. In a separate bowl, stir together mayonnaise, sugar, and vinegar. Add to broccoli mixture, stirring well to combine. Cover and refrigerate. Makes 2 quarts.

Potato Salad

VELMA'S DINER, SHOALS
Debbie Montgomery

Some potato salad recipes call for mayonnaise, others use salad dressing, and some use neither. Debbie, who makes this by the panful, is firmly in the salad dressing camp and prefers Miracle Whip brand. "I don't like mayonnaise," she says. "I really don't know why."

5 **pounds potatoes**
1¹⁄₂ **cups salad dressing (such as Miracle Whip brand)**
1 **tablespoon mustard**
1 **tablespoon sweet pickle relish**
6 **hard-cooked eggs, chopped**
¹⁄₂ **cup diced onion**
   salt and pepper to taste

Boil potatoes until tender; drain. When cool enough to handle, peel and dice potatoes.

Stir together salad dressing, mustard, and relish in large bowl. Add potatoes, eggs, and onion, stirring well to combine. Season to taste with salt and pepper. Cover and refrigerate. Serves 12.

(continued from facing page)

one of the large dinner plates on the hot food side of the smorgasbord.

I plunged in with abandon, piling a token mound of crispy iceberg lettuce onto the center of the plate, then adding shredded carrots, sliced cucumbers, rings of green pepper, bite-size pieces of cauliflower and broccoli florets, tomato wedges, sliced fresh mushrooms, and diced onion. Around the edge of the plate I spooned dollops of specialty salads: coleslaw, potato salad, ambrosia made with coconut and mandarin oranges, kidney bean salad, cauliflower, broccoli and carrot salad, pea salad, and apple Waldorf salad.

Did I mention it was all homemade? No jars opened and dumped onto this buffet, which I hereby anoint the queen of Hoosier salad bars. —J.S., adapted from *Cafe Indiana*

Bean Salad

HIGHWAY 341 COUNTRY CAFE, WALLACE
Tony and Linda Shuman

No family reunion or church pitch-in is complete without bean salad, and it's always available as a side dish at the combination cafe and opry hall in tiny Wallace. "We seldom run out because we can make it up right quick," says Tony. "The longer it sits, the better it is."

>   2 (15-ounce) cans kidney beans, drained
>   2 hard-cooked eggs, chopped
>   ½ cup diced onion
>   ½ cup chopped celery
>   ¼ cup salad dressing (such as Miracle Whip brand)
>   2 tablespoons pickle relish
>   sugar, salt, and pepper

In a medium bowl, combine beans, eggs, onion, and celery. Stir together salad dressing and relish; add to bean mixture, stirring well to combine. Season to taste with sugar, salt, and pepper. Cover and refrigerate. Serves 6.

Cook's note: For extra flavor, drizzle with balsamic vinegar.

Macaroni Salad

BOBBIE JO'S DINER, EDINBURGH
Bobbie Jo Hart

This is a forgiving salad to make; simply taste as you go and make adjustments accordingly. Prefer a little more mayo or a little less pickle relish (or dill pickle relish over the sweet variety)? No problem. But Bertha Burton, the master cook at Bobbie Jo's Diner, does insist on finely diced ingredients. For potato salad, substitute diced potatoes for the macaroni.

>   2 cups elbow macaroni
>   ½ cup finely diced celery
>   ½ cup finely diced onion
>   3 hard-cooked eggs, finely chopped
>   2 tablespoons sweet pickle relish
>   ½ cup mayonnaise

1 **tablespoon yellow mustard**
   sugar, salt, and pepper

Cook macaroni according to package directions; drain and rinse under cold water. Place drained macaroni in a bowl. Add remaining ingredients, stirring to combine. Refrigerate to allow flavors to blend. Serves 4.

Restaurant-Style Coleslaw

OLD SCHOOL CAFE, PLEASANT
Roger and Dawn Christman

Coleslaw can be tart and vinegary or sweet and creamy. This is definitely the sweet and creamy variety, and it's a favorite among customers at the Old School Cafe.

1¼ **cups sugar**
  2 **tablespoons vegetable oil**
  2 **tablespoons plus 1½ teaspoons white vinegar**
  2 **cups mayonnaise (such as Hellmann's brand)**
1½ **tablespoons seasoned salt**
  2 **teaspoons black pepper**
  2 **teaspoons ground celery seed**
1½ **medium heads cabbage, shredded**
  1 **medium carrot, shredded**

In a medium bowl, stir together sugar and vegetable oil; add vinegar. Stir in mayonnaise; add seasoned salt, pepper, and celery seed. Set aside.

Combine shredded cabbage and carrots in a large bowl, tossing until well mixed. Add mayonnaise mixture, stirring well to coat. Cover and refrigerate until ready to serve. Serves 12.

Bloom Where You're Planted

As a longtime caterer, Ann Cain hoped to experiment with a variety of foods at the Wolcott Theatre Cafe, which she opened in the lobby of the town's former movie theater in 2004. Instead, she quickly discovered that her menu had to be "customer driven." She wanted chicken cordon bleu. They wanted chicken-fried steak. "I hoped it would be a little more gourmet," she admits, "but that's maybe a little bit of a dream not realized." She sticks with tried and true comfort food like chicken and noodles, lasagna, biscuits and gravy, and ultra-deep-dish pies and fruit cobblers, conceding that her regular customers "are pretty happy with the predictability." Even the drop-ins from Chicago, whom she regards as generally very "experienced eaters," demand "food like what Grandma made," she

(continued on facing page)

Marinated Vegetable Bowl

Wolcott Theatre Cafe, Wolcott
Ann Cain

An excellent way to use fresh-from-the-garden produce, these marinated vegetables look great on the table. This is Ann's most oft-requested recipe. She came up with the dish to showcase fresh, gorgeous vegetables; use whatever is in season. "Pick what appeals to your senses," she says.

      16-ounce bottle Italian dressing
$\frac{1}{4}$ **cup sugar or Splenda**
$\frac{1}{4}$ **cup fresh chopped herbs, such as cilantro, dill, or chives**
  1 **medium cucumber, cut in chunks**
  2 **bell peppers, red, green, yellow, or combination, cut in chunks**
  1 **pint cherry tomatoes**
  1 **bunch green onions, chopped**
  1 **cup fresh green beans, in inch-long pieces**
  1 **cup broccoli and cauliflower florets**
  1 **cup sugar snap peas**
  1 **cup chopped carrots**

Combine Italian dressing with sugar and herbs. Place in lidded jar, cover, and shake well. Place cucumber and pepper chunks, tomatoes, and onions in a large bowl; add dressing and toss to coat.

Prepare a large bowl with ice water. In a steamer, cook remaining vegetables just until crisp-tender. Place vegetables immediately in ice water bath and cool for 5 minutes. Drain well and add to vegetables with dressing, tossing well. Chill before serving. Serves 6.

Tuna or Chicken Salad

VICKY'S RESTAURANT, WINAMAC
Vicky and Dave Pingel

Vicky has made these salads since she was young. They're served year round, she says, "not only for sandwiches, but for stuffed tomatoes as well—only we use sliced tomatoes; it's easier to eat that way."

> 3 (6.4-ounce) pouches tuna (such as StarKist) or
>   2 cups cooked chicken
> 4 hard-cooked eggs, finely chopped
> ½ cup finely chopped celery
> ¼ cup finely chopped diced onion
> ½ to 1 teaspoon celery seed
> 3 tablespoons salad dressing (such as Miracle Whip),
>   or to taste
> 1 to 2 tablespoons sweet pickle relish, or to taste

In a medium bowl, separate tuna or shred chicken. Combine with remaining ingredients, adjusting amounts to desired taste and consistency. Serve as sandwiches or atop sliced tomatoes. Serves 6.

Pickled Eggs and Beets

MARTY'S BLUEBIRD CAFE, LAKETON
Martha "Marty" and Bart Huffman

These fuschia-colored eggs add old-fashioned flavor to any meal. "Bart's mom makes these for me on special occasions," says Marty.

> 1 (15-ounce) can sliced beets, undrained
> ¼ cup sugar
> ½ cup vinegar
> 6 hard-cooked eggs

In a medium saucepan, heat beets with sugar and vinegar, stirring until sugar dissolves.

Place eggs in a shallow, lidded bowl. Pour beet mixture over eggs. Cover and refrigerate two days before serving. Serve the beets and eggs separately, if desired. Serves 4 to 6.

(continued from facing page)

says. "So you gotta kind of bloom where you're planted. That means a lot of chicken-fried steak."

Ann orchestrates small victories over the routine by sneaking in new items, like her Italian marinated vegetable salad, that quickly become customer favorites. "How many times can I serve beans and corn? People eat the salad and don't even realize they're eating vegetables."—J.S., adapted from *Cafe Indiana*

IF IT'S NOT BROKE . . .

With an average age of fifty and older—perhaps the last generation to have grown up on "old-fashioned farm cooking"—the regulars at Marty's Bluebird Cafe in Laketon stick like glue to the tried and true. "This is a meat and potatoes place," says Marty Huffman, co-owner with her husband, Bart. "People here like their meat loaf. Anything out of the ordinary—well! Oh, my gosh!" Not surprisingly, from sunrise opening to early-afternoon close, Marty concentrates on traditional Hoosier home cooking, like real mashed potatoes ("I always leave lumps in them so you know"), beef and noodles, tenderloins, biscuits and gravy, fried cornmeal mush, and desserts ranging from summertime ice cream treats to "occasionally a cake."

Fancy schmancy, Marty has found, just doesn't sell. "I get bored and kind of aggravated because they want only that old-home cooking. We'd love to get away from all of the noodles and grease—not that the food's greasy!—but they're just not receptive to that. If it's not burgers and noodles, they don't want it." She finds ways to flex her creative muscle and slip in more exciting fare, however. For a few years, she and Bart prepared a Valentine's Day gourmet candlelight dinner. One year they served rabbit. Another year they prepared grilled pork ribs rubbed with herbs and spices. Though the dinners were never in great demand, Marty hoped that the locals' gentle introduction to alternative dining could pave the way to nightly experiences with "finer, more experimental foods" once Bart retired. "We thought about opening at night to share our passion about food," she says, but their dream never materialized. "I've kind of learned from trying not to zing things up with spices. It's a real struggle some times. But you put a coney dog in front of them, and they'll fight you to the bone."—J.S., adapted from *Cafe Indiana*

Pineapple Cheese Salad

Liz's Country Cafe, North Salem
Liz Freeland

This unusual salad featuring thickened pineapple juice, pineapple chunks, mini marshmallows, and cheese can be found in a handful of cafes in central Indiana. Some substitute sliced processed American cheese, Velveeta, or shredded cheddar. If you spot this salad on a cafe salad bar, don't assume, as Joanne did when she first encountered it, that cheese had somehow fallen in by mistake. It's supposed to be in there.

> 2 **(20-ounce) cans chunk pineapple in juice**
> 1 **cup sugar**
> 2 **tablespoons cornstarch**
> 1 **egg yolk, beaten**
> 4 **ounces cheddar cheese, cut into bite-size cubes**
> 1 **cup mini marshmallows**

Drain juice from 1 can of pineapple chunks into small saucepan (discard juice from remaining can, or reserve for another use). Mix sugar and cornstarch and add to juice. Add egg yolk; cook, stirring, until thick. Remove from heat and cool to room temperature.

Combine cheese, pineapple, and marshmallows in medium bowl. Add thickened juice, stirring to combine. Refrigerate. Serve chilled. Serves 6.

Cranberry Salad

PALMER HOUSE, BERNE

Sharon and Roger LeFever and Saundra and Keith Minger

Cranberries aren't just for Thanksgiving. This rosy salad can be found on the salad table during the legendary Friday night all-you-can-eat buffet at Palmer House. If you have a grinder attachment for your mixer, avoid the chopping and simply grind the apples and orange together.

- 3 (4-ounce) boxes cherry-flavored gelatin
- ¾ cup sugar
- 3 cups hot water
- 1¼ cups orange juice
- 2½ cups jelly-style cranberry sauce
- 3 apples, diced
- 1 orange, diced
- 1 cup chopped celery
- 3 cups chopped nuts

Mix together gelatin, sugar, and hot water, stirring well until dissolved. Add orange juice and cranberry sauce. Stir in remaining ingredients. Cover and refrigerate. Serves 12.

Apple Salad

CHAMBERS SMORGASBORD, SPENCER

Barbara Chambers and Jim Chambers

You might recognize this recipe as a variation of Waldorf salad, an American classic that is more than a century old. Barbara got the recipe from her mother-in-law, Violet, who ran a small restaurant at the entrance of McCormick's Creek State Park in the 1950s.

- 4 red Delicious apples
- ¾ cup chopped celery
- ½ cup chopped walnuts
- ½ cup mini marshmallows
- ¾ cup mayonnaise
- ¼ cup sugar, or less to taste

Core and cut apples into bite-size pieces. In a medium bowl, combine apples, celery, walnuts, and marshmallows. Stir together mayonnaise and sugar. Add to apple mixture, stirring well to combine. Serves 4.

Pear Salad with Orange Pecan Dressing

CAFE MAX, CULVER
Susie Mahler

This salad is a great starter to a meal, or top it with grilled chicken breast for lunch or a light supper. "We wanted to create a lighter salad and came up with this one," says assistant manager Wendy Van Horn. At Cafe Max, this salad is served with a generous chunk of home-baked wheat bread and sweet whipped butter.

- 2 cups vegetable oil
- 2 cups orange juice
- ½ cup honey
- 1 cup chopped pecans, divided
- 1 teaspoon dry mustard
- 1 teaspoon celery salt
- 16 ounces mixed greens
- 1 pear, sliced thin
- ½ cup dried cranberries
- ½ cup crumbled blue cheese

In a lidded jar, combine vegetable oil, orange juice, honey, ½ cup pecans, mustard, and celery salt. Cover and shake to mix.

Toss greens with dressing. Evenly distribute dressed greens among four wide-rimmed plates or bowls. Evenly space pear segments around rims. Sprinkle each with crumbled blue cheese, dried cranberries, and remaining ½ cup chopped pecans. Serves 4.

WHAT WAS OLD IS NEW AGAIN

Due to the presence of the independent Culver Academies, whose students come from moneyed families, and millionaires who have erected palatial homes on Lake Maxinkuckee, Culver is a peculiar and enticing mixture of traditional small-town culture and urban sophistication. The two-block commercial district, which has begun to enjoy a spirited renewal, perfectly represents the mix. Anchoring the south end of Main Street is Culver Pro Hardware, a workaday source of an assortment of necessities to keep both utilitarian houses and summer villas running without a hitch. It is joined by a scattering of clever little shops selling gifts, fancy antiques and collectibles, and upscale clothing that survive on the pocketbooks of Culver's seasonal residents and visitors.

Culver native Susie Mahler has made Cafe Max a happy meeting ground for everyone who calls Culver home—both full time and part time—and for plenty of others who don't. Worn out by the heat and too many miles on the road, and with the discovery of a truly remarkable cafe long overdue, I step inside Cafe Max with considerable expectation. And though I have been told that the cafe doubles as a local museum featuring town, academy, and Lake Maxinkuckee history, I am not altogether prepared for the collection of wonderful stuff that I encounter. There are Culver High School marching band uniforms and tasseled hats (and a yellowed bass drum from the old junior high), framed historic photos, letter sweaters and yell sweaters, athletic trophies and discarded academy uniforms with insignia and badges and tassels and medals. But my hands-down, without-a-doubt favorite is a corduroy skirt with an impossibly small waist suspended from the ceiling above my table. It is the senior cords of Mimi Miller, a member of the Culver High School class of 1962. The cream-colored skirt is painted with color caricatures of a lanky basketball player (number 3) and Mimi's chums, whose signatures testify to their undying friendship.

All this old is actually new. When Susie bought the town cafe in 1985 and began ridding it of its dated 1970s appearance, her remodeling was at first not well received. Susie remembers, "My customers were cost conscious for me. They warned me that the high ceiling would mean high heating bills. They were concerned that I was going backward."

Though they were fearful of falling into the past, it was the very same customers who suggested that history—in the form of memorabilia from Culver's own past—be used to decorate the emerging restaurant. Embracing the idea, Susie concentrated on three themes that have defined Culver through the years: town, academy, and lake. The cafe's collection got a

considerable boost when the old high school was replaced by a new build-ing, and items that had been in storage since 1968 were transferred to Cafe Max. That was the year that Culver High School merged with area township schools to form the Culver Community Schools system. "The photos were taken down and the school colors changed from maroon and white to orange and black," Susie explains. "I guess they wanted to start fresh, so they put all of that old stuff in storage. We're fortunate that they saved it and we have it today." —J.S., adapted from *Cafe Indiana*

Healthy Quinoa Summer Salad

Hilltop Restaurant, Lakeville

Karen Iovino and Vera Gouker

Quinoa (pronounced keen-wah) is a South American grain and a great source of protein. The mild-flavored grain cooks quickly, mak-ing it easy to toss together this flavorful salad. Look for quinoa with the packaged grains at the grocery store; Bob's Red Mill is a common brand.

- 1 **cup quinoa, rinsed**
- 2 **cups water**
- 1 **cup canned chickpeas, drained and rinsed**
- 1 **tomato, seeded and chopped**
- 1 **(13.75-ounce) can quartered artichoke hearts, drained**
-    **sliced olives, chopped bell pepper, and sliced green onions, if desired**
-    **salt and pepper**
- ¾ **cup bottled Italian dressing, or to taste**
-    **chopped fresh parsley**

Combine quinoa and water in a saucepan; bring to a boil, cover and simmer 10 minutes.

In a large bowl, combine chickpeas, tomato, and artichoke hearts. Add olives, bell pepper, and green onions, if using. Add quinoa. Sea-son to taste with salt and pepper. Stir in Italian dressing; garnish with chopped parsley. Cover and refrigerate to allow flavors to blend. Serve cold or at room temperature.

Sweet and Sour Dressing

CORNER CAFE, WAKARUSA
Candy and Alan Krull

A gallon of this versatile dressing is used every week at the Corner Cafe. "I use it for stir-fry dressing," says Candy's mom Marsha, who serves it alongside sautéed vegetables, chicken, and almond rice. "It is also used as a salad dressing and a dip for bread."

$2\frac{1}{2}$ cups sugar
$\frac{3}{4}$ cup apple cider vinegar
$1\frac{1}{2}$ cups vegetable oil
$\frac{1}{2}$ cup mayonnaise
$\frac{1}{4}$ cup yellow mustard
$\frac{3}{4}$ teaspoon pepper
$\frac{3}{4}$ teaspoon celery seed

Combine sugar, vinegar, and vegetable oil in a medium saucepan. Cook over medium heat, stirring, until sugar dissolves. Boil, stirring occasionally, for 5 minutes.

Meanwhile, stir together mayonnaise, mustard, pepper, and celery seed in a bowl. Pour hot mixture over mayonnaise mixture, stirring until well blended. Cool, cover, and refrigerate. Serve over stir-fried vegetables or salad or use as dip for raw vegetables or crusty bread. Makes 5 cups.

Honey Mustard Dressing

OLD SCHOOL CAFE, PLEASANT
Roger and Dawn Christman

This is head cook Judy May's own creation. It's great over salad or as a dipping sauce.

1 cup mayonnaise (such as Hellmann's brand)
$\frac{1}{4}$ cup yellow mustard
$1\frac{1}{2}$ teaspoons paprika
$1\frac{1}{2}$ teaspoons chili powder
scant $\frac{1}{2}$ cup honey

Combine all ingredients. Cover and refrigerate until using. Makes $1\frac{3}{4}$ cups.

FIVE

~ ~ ~

Sides and Extras

Yeast Rolls

HIGHWAY 341 COUNTRY CAFE, WALLACE
Tony and Linda Shuman

Tony spent a year refining his yeast roll recipe. "I just remembered how Mom used to do some of this stuff and tried to figure it out," he says. "Mother's were probably three times bigger than what I made, and she made them by hand." Twenty to thirty dozen rolls will be served on Friday and Saturday nights when the cafe is packed from wall to wall for live country music by Tony's own Highway 341 Band.

1 1/2 **cups water**
1 1/2 **cups sugar**
  2 **teaspoons salt**
 1/2 **cup butter**
  1 **cup warm water**
 1/4 **cup yeast (not fast rising)**
4 to 6 **cups flour**
 1/4 **cup butter, melted**

In a saucepan, combine 1 1/2 cups water with the sugar, salt, and 1/2 cup butter and cook over medium heat until mixture comes to a boil; let cool to room temperature.

To the cup of warm water, add the yeast, stirring well to combine. In bowl of a stand mixer fitted with a dough hook, combine yeast with room temperature liquid. Add flour, a little at a time, until dough pulls away from sides of mixing bowl. Turn dough into large, lightly oiled mixing bowl, turning once to coat. Place in draft-free area, cover with clean kitchen towel, and allow to rise until doubled in size, about an hour, punching down twice.

Spray jumbo-size muffin pans, including the top of pan, with nonstick cooking spray. To make rolls, pinch off small amounts of dough and shape in golf ball–size balls. Place 2 balls in each cup of muffin pans, cover, and let rise again, about an hour. Bake at 350 degrees for 15 minutes. Remove from oven and brush with melted butter. Makes 2 dozen.

ROCKIN' NIGHTS IN WALLACE

A Fountain County farming community of about ninety residents, Wallace is the kind of place you're more likely to drive through than drive to. The downtown—the whole town actually—consists of a post office, lodge hall, fire station, Model T garage, a handful of houses, and the cafe that Tony and Linda Shuman purchased in 2003. Tony retired after forty years of installing commercial refrigerators, moved back home to Indiana from Alabama, and fulfilled a dream of running his own home cooking–style restaurant and making music on the side.

Tony was a member of popular local bands during the sixties and seventies, and, as a member of Jade, recorded a version of "Chattanooga Shoe Shine Boy" that was a *Billboard* magazine country honorable mention in June 1984. "Two years later I moved out of state, and the music stopped. Then I went to Alabama and met a couple of musicians and started jamming around a little bit. And the music came back," he says.

In 2003, the Shumans bought the Wallace general store and cafe and set about converting the old building into a music hall that packs 'em in every Thursday and Saturday night beginning with dinner at 4:30 p.m. It's as unlikely a little place as you're apt to find in a speck of a town like Wallace.

Tip #1: Reservations are an absolute must. Do not expect to wander in off the street and find a place to sit, let alone stand. The Highway 341 Cafe really rocks, mostly with folks in their sixties and seventies who wouldn't consider missing a night unless there was a death in the family.

Tip #2: Be sure to put in your dibs for pie early or you will be disappointed. It will sell out. I'm told that the pie "is the biggest and cheapest," and that's right. Half a piece of lemon meringue is all I could comfortably manage after a meal of beef Manhattan for dinner.

Tip #3: Expect a whole lot of fun. The regulars are so at home in the Highway 341 Cafe that they have no reason at all to be self-conscious. Their zany goofiness is an infectious delight. You, too, may find yourself on the dance floor, arms crooked and flapping like chicken wings.

Tip #4: Wear comfortable shoes. Cars from two states stretch along the highway two blocks in either direction, which means you'll have a hike to reach the cafe. Wallace hasn't experienced this kind of activity for years. "If Tony and Linda didn't come here, Wallace wouldn't be here," says Allen Heyworth, one of the music night regulars. —J.S., adapted from *Cafe Indiana*

Southern-Style Corn Bread

Corn bread is another of those recipes that we just had to include, even though no cafe owner offered one. It could be that knowing how to make cornbread is just taken for granted. Here is the recipe that Jolene turns to when corn bread is called for. Lacking sugar, this cornbread is savory, not sweet, and baked in the traditional southern way in a heavily greased skillet. It is a must alongside Hoosier ham and beans but is also terrific spread with butter.

In the Appalachian mountains, from which many of Indiana's early settlers came, corn bread is much more than a food staple. "Corn bread is so popular and so important that some mountaineers view it as a gift from God," writes Mark F. Sohn in *Appalachian Home Cooking*.

> 1 cup cornmeal
> ¼ cup flour
> 3 teaspoons baking powder
> 1 teaspoon salt
> 1 egg
> 1 cup milk
> 3 tablespoons shortening, melted

Stir together cornmeal, flour, baking powder, and salt. Break egg into milk, stirring to combine; add to dry ingredients.

Melt shortening in 10-inch cast-iron skillet, making sure sides of skillet are well greased. Pour shortening into cornmeal mixture; stir well to combine. Pour mixture into skillet. Bake for 30 minutes at 350 degrees until golden brown. Serves 6.

Northern-Style Corn Bread

The addition of sugar and an extra egg makes a lighter, sweeter corn-bread more typical of the northern states. This is why it is sometimes called Yankee cornbread. Joanne uses this recipe, which she got from her Wisconsin mother-in-law. She uses only stone-ground yellow cornmeal sold at Spring Mill State Park. These muffins once won a blue ribbon at the Morgan County Fair.

$\frac{1}{3}$ **cup sugar**
$\frac{1}{2}$ **cup butter, melted**
  2 **eggs**
$1\frac{1}{2}$ **cups yellow cornmeal**
$1\frac{1}{2}$ **cups flour**
  $\frac{3}{4}$ **teaspoon salt**
$1\frac{1}{2}$ **cup buttermilk**
  1 **teaspoon baking soda**
  3 **teaspoons baking powder**

Combine sugar, butter, and slightly beaten eggs. Combine cornmeal, flour, and salt. Add egg mixture to dry mixture and stir. Add baking soda and baking powder to buttermilk and stir well. Mix buttermilk mixture to cornmeal mixture and stir until moistened. Bake in well-greased muffin pans at 400 degrees for 15 to 20 minutes. Makes 12 to 16 muffins.

BISCUITS

Biscuits are a break-fast staple in Indiana's cafes and usually appear covered in sausage gravy. But in southern Indiana, biscuits are often deep fried and served with apple butter. Popularized by Brown County's Nashville House restaurant, fried biscuits and apple butter have become popular across the state. You'll even see them served alongside fried chicken and corn on the cob at catered events surrounding the Indianapolis 500-Mile Race. While canned refrigerated biscuits are often used for deep frying, here are a couple of my favorite biscuit recipes. They're perfect with gravy or slathered with butter or jam. —J.K.

Mile-High Biscuits 🏁

Although a lot of folks use canned, biscuits made from scratch are a home-cooking classic we had to include despite not receiving a recipe for them. With egg and baking powder this recipe yields a high-rising biscuit; it's also a bit sweet. Be sure to knead only briefly and use a sharp biscuit cutter. When cutting out biscuits, avoid twisting the cutter; the biscuits will rise higher if you use a straight-down cutting motion. And for the lightest, fluffiest biscuits, use a brand of low-protein, low-gluten flour milled from soft wheat, such as long-time southern favorite White Lily. The flour had been milled since 1883 in Knoxville, Tennessee, but the brand was bought by the J. M. Smucker Company, and the flour is now produced in midwestern mills.

> 3 **cups flour**
> 4½ **teaspoons baking powder**
> ¾ **teaspoon cream of tartar**
> 2½ **tablespoons sugar**
> ¾ **teaspoon salt**
> ¾ **cup shortening**
> 1 **egg**
> 1 **cup milk**

Preheat oven to 450 degrees. Grease baking sheet. Mix dry ingredients. Cut in shortening. Beat egg slightly; add to milk. Add egg and milk mixture to dry ingredients and mix with fork until dough holds together. Turn out onto floured board and knead lightly. Roll dough to 1-inch thick. Cut out biscuits with 2-inch round cookie cutter. Place on prepared sheet and bake for 12 minutes or until light brown. Makes 2 dozen.

Baking Powder Biscuits

This recipe is a bit quicker and a bit more savory. With no sugar and a bit more salt, it lends itself well to that hearty breakfast favorite, biscuits and gravy. These also make great little ham sandwiches; you can even mix your favorite herb into the dough before baking. But if you prefer your biscuits with butter and jam, these work fine for that as well.

- 2 **cups flour**
- 3 **teaspoons baking powder**
- 1 **teaspoon salt**
- 3½ **tablespoons shortening**
- ⅔ **cup milk**

Preheat oven to 450 degrees. Mix and sift dry ingredients. Cut in shortening. Add milk gradually, stirring to combine. Turn out onto floured board and knead lightly. Roll dough to ½-inch thick. Cut out biscuits with 2-inch round cookie cutter. Place on ungreased cookie sheet and bake for 15 minutes or until light brown. Makes 1½ dozen.

Fried Biscuits

This is one of those recipes that doesn't really need a recipe—it's just that common. Traditionally served with apple butter, fried biscuits have become a southern Indiana specialty. Canned biscuits are typically used, but the biscuit dough can also be homemade. If you don't have apple butter, sprinkle them with powdered sugar or a mix of cinnamon and sugar.

- 3 **cups vegetable oil for frying**
- 1 **can refrigerated biscuits**
  apple butter

In a deep, heavy pan, heat oil to 350 degrees. Carefully drop in biscuits, a few at a time, and fry for approximately 3 minutes or until evenly brown. Drain on paper towels; serve immediately with apple butter. Makes 10 biscuits.

Apple Butter

CHAMBERS SMORGASBORD, SPENCER
Barbara Chambers and Jim Chambers

This recipe comes from Barbara's mother-in-law, Violet Chambers. It's been made at Chambers for nearly forty years and never has a day off. From morning to night, you can spread it on fresh baked white and wheat bread or scoop it up with hot fried biscuits. It's a so-good taste of the Hoosier hills in Spencer, where the Owen County Apple Butter Festival is held every September.

1 **(50-ounce) jar applesauce**
1 **cup brown sugar, heaped**
1 **tablespoon cinnamon**
2 **ounces cinnamon red hot candies**

With a wire whisk, mix applesauce, brown sugar, cinnamon, and red hots. Pour into a large baking dish. Bake at 350 degrees for 6 to 7 hours, stirring occasionally. Remove from oven and stir well. Serve with fried biscuits, if desired. It's also delicious spread on toast, English muffins, or regular biscuits.

Deviled Eggs 🏴

A choice of two side dishes commonly accompanies a cafe's daily special, and you're likely to find this simple favorite on the specials board. It is equally popular at family picnics and church pitch-ins and almost always disappears quickly. Jolene provides this recipe in the absence of one sent in by cafe owners.

Feel free to adjust the ingredients to taste—some may prefer more mustard or none at all, while others swear by the addition of sweet pickle relish. A sprinkling of paprika makes an appealing presentation.

 6 **large hard-boiled eggs, peeled and halved**
 3 **tablespoons mayonnaise (or to taste)**
 1 **teaspoon mustard (or to taste)**
   salt and pepper
   paprika

Remove yolks from whites, placing yolks in a medium bowl; reserve whites. Add mayonnaise and mustard to yolks and mash with a fork until smooth and well mixed. Season to taste with salt and pepper. Spoon mixture into whites; sprinkle with paprika. Serves 6.

Roesti

PALMER HOUSE, BERNE
Sharon and Roger LeFever and Saundra and Keith Minger

Roesti, an extra-good version of fried potatoes, was brought to Berne and the surrounding area by German-speaking Swiss Mennonite immigrants in the mid-nineteenth century. Today, it is sometimes considered to be a Swiss national dish. Boiling and chilling the potatoes beforehand makes them lighter and crispier when fried.

 4 **medium potatoes**
 1 **medium onion, chopped**
 2 **tablespoons vegetable oil plus more as needed**

Boil potatoes until tender; drain and chill until completely cold. Slip skins from potatoes and slice very thin, using a slicer or mandoline.

In a large nonstick skillet, heat oil over medium heat until very hot. Carefully add potatoes and chopped onions and cook, stirring, until potatoes are crisp and browned. Serves 4.

Playing Swiss in Berne

Polka music is playing over the town loudspeakers when I pull into Berne a week after the annual Swiss Days Festival has ended. At five thirty in the afternoon, the town looks deserted. The Palmer House is, too, with the exception of owner Saundra Minger and her daughter and granddaughter, who are enjoying a quiet dinner.

"It's a good thing you didn't come last week," Saundra says. "I wouldn't have had a minute to sit down with you."

Saundra has lived in Adams County her entire life, so she has been both an observer and a participant in Berne's transformation from a fairly typical Hoosier farm community to a Little Switzerland. Settled by Swiss Mennonites in 1852 and today a commercial hub of thriving Mennonite and orthodox Amish communities, Berne began promoting its Swiss heritage in the early 1970s. Business owners were persuaded to remodel their buildings in a Swiss chalet style complete with folk art adornment and window boxes, and an annual festival was added to the calendar. "The festival started out as a town sidewalk sale," recalls Saundra. Over the years it has evolved into a popular three-day festival featuring Bavarian music, folk dancing, tours of a nearby Swiss-themed living history museum, a community musical performance titled *In Grand Old Switzerland*, street activities, and much more.

According to the Web site of the Berne Chamber of Commerce, "Berne offers the discovery of historic nostalgia" with old-world hospitality, quaintness, friendly people, and "authentic Swiss architecture." Berne's traditions are not preserved and handed down from generation to generation, however. They are reinventions of traditions, of Swiss things rethought, reconfigured, and revived in a new time and place. They are not "historic nostalgia" but rather nostalgia that has been romantically historicized.

While Berne plays at being Swiss, real tradition and history merge in authentic and meaningful ways at the Palmer House, a landmark restaurant opened in 1939 by Ralph Liechty, a Swiss with the unlikely nickname of Gandhi. Palmer Liechty followed in the 1940s, renaming the restaurant Palmer House and redecorating it in the fashion of midcentury. This meant a good supply of natural birch cabinets with chrome handles, white Formica tabletops spattered with gold flecks, and a pair of horseshoe counters banded with wide blue stripes. This is the Palmer House today. This is history *and* tradition that remains hard at work.

The everyday menu continues to include traditional Swiss-style foods that Saundra and her co-owner, Sharon LeFever, grew up on. Schweizer

salad is a bowl of iceberg lettuce, sliced hard-cooked eggs, bacon chips, and hot bacon dressing. The best-selling Swiss steak is, according to Saundra, "round steak, tenderized, floured, baked, and served with glop." Hummel Fummel is a heavenly fruit dessert (see recipe on page 136), heiße Kartoffelsalat is hot potato salad, and the mysterious roesti nothing other than crispy potato pancakes. Saundra notes that among the traditional Swiss foods, nothing is so unusual as to be exotic. "The Swiss just made good, common food: meat, potatoes, and vegetables."—J.S., adapted from *Cafe Indiana*

Fried Green Tomatoes

VELMA'S DINER, SHOALS
Debbie Montgomery

Customers at Velma's Diner start asking for this popular side long before tomato season. When plants are bursting with bounty—local gardeners sometimes deliver them by the bagful—fried green tomatoes are often ordered as a stand-alone dish; some customers make a sandwich out of them. "They are so popular," says Debbie, "it's hard to keep up with the orders."

- 6 **large green tomatoes**
- 2 **cups cornmeal**
- 1 **cup flour**
  salt and pepper to taste
- 1 **cup water**
  vegetable oil for frying

Slice tomatoes in $\frac{1}{2}$-inch slices. In a shallow bowl, combine cornmeal, flour, salt, and pepper.

Dip tomato slices, one at a time, into water. Coat in cornmeal mixture, shaking off excess, and place slices on plate.

In a large skillet, heat 1 inch of vegetable oil until hot. Carefully add tomato slices to skillet in a single layer; do not crowd. Working in batches, and adding more oil as necessary, fry tomato slices until golden and crisp, turning once. Drain on paper towels. Serve immediately. Serves 4 to 6.

Green Beans

HIGHWAY 341 COUNTRY CAFE, WALLACE
Tony and Linda Shuman

This is a real down-home recipe, a side dish served almost every day at Highway 341 Country Cafe. "Mom made them like this," says Tony. "Mom was just an old-time cook, basically, and that's how we growed up." If you happen to have leftover baked potatoes, use them up with this recipe as Tony does. Fresh green beans will require a longer time to cook.

> 1 **large baking potato**
> 2 **teaspoons cooking oil or baking grease**
> ½ **cup diced onion**
> ½ **cup ham, chopped, or crumbled cooked bacon**
> 3 **(14.5-ounce) cans green beans**
>   **salt and pepper to taste**

Microwave potato until barely tender. When cool enough to handle, peel potato and cut into chunks.

Heat oil in small skillet. Sauté onion with ham until onions are soft and translucent.

In a medium saucepan, combine green beans with potato, onions, and ham. Bring to a simmer and cook until potatoes are completely tender. Season with salt and pepper. Serves 6.

Tomato Gravy

WOLCOTT THEATRE CAFE, WOLCOTT
Ann Cain

Ann says this is a family recipe that was used often during World War II, served over biscuits or toast points. "It's a great old standby that deserves to be revived." The economical dish also derives from Appalachian, Amish, and Pennsylvania Dutch culinary traditions.

- ½ **pound bacon, diced**
- 1 **small onion, diced**
- 2 **tablespoons flour**
- ½ **teaspoon salt**
- ¼ **teaspoon pepper**
- 1 **(14.5-ounce) can diced tomatoes**
- 3 **cups tomato juice**

In a large skillet, cook bacon until crisp; remove and drain. Add onion and cook until tender. Stir in flour, salt, and pepper. Cook over low heat, stirring, until golden brown. Gradually add tomatoes and tomato juice, stirring well. Bring to a boil, then cook 15 minutes until thickened, stirring occasionally. Stir in bacon. Serve over biscuits, toast, fried cornmeal mush, or pasta. Serves 6.

APPALACHIA ON MY PLATE

Much of Indiana's food heritage can be traced to the southern mountains from which many of the state's early settlers came. The Appalachian region stretches from northeastern Alabama up into New York and Pennsylvania, but it is the highland area along the borders of Tennessee, Kentucky, North Carolina, and Virginia that contributed so much to Indiana's cultural history. The myth of the lone and rugged pioneer often has him traipsing into new lands with nothing more than an ax thrown over his shoulder. But he brought so much more than that. He brought all kinds of cultural knowledge: patterns of speech, specific types of houses and barns, bluegrass music, Quakerism, and, of course, foods.

Mark F. Sohn, a professor at Pikeville College in Kentucky, has spent years exploring the unique eats of Appalachia. In *Appalachian Home Cooking*, he offers a list of the "top ten most authentic Appalachian foods" in order of importance. Tops is chicken and dumplings, followed by corn bread, apple stack cake, biscuits and sausage gravy, soup beans, fried potatoes, pork chops, fried chicken, deviled eggs, and green beans. If we move apple stack cake, a true mountain specialty, a bit lower down on the list, what we have is pure Hoosier. Hoosier down to its Appalachian core.

The southern highlands were settled by English, Scot, and Irish colonists moving westward, away from the eastern seaboard. Because the mountains were so thickly wooded and remote, these early settlers remained culturally isolated. According to Sohn, today's everyday foods—potatoes, biscuits, dumplings, buttermilk, gravy, even apple pie—suggest a strong connection with the British Isles.

In the mid-nineteenth century, the removal of coal, timber, and other natural resources brought workers from a variety of cultural backgrounds to the region, and food naturally became more diverse. The popularity of pork (ham, bacon, sausage, chops, souse), beans (green and dried), and corn (including corn bread), plus other garden vegetables and fruits, and foods from other nationalities derives from the frontier and industrial periods of Appalachian settlement.

Down through the generations, these foods have become classics of Hoosier home cooking—and you'll likely find plenty of them at any small-town cafe. —J.S.

Macaroni and Tomatoes

JULIE'S TELL STREET CAFE, TELL CITY
Julie Fischer

This simple side is served only on Mondays, Julie tells us. But what to order as a main dish? "It goes well with meat loaf," she says.

2 cups elbow macaroni
2 (14.5-ounce) cans diced tomatoes with onions and
       green peppers
    salt and pepper
    tomato juice or V-8 juice if necessary

Cook macaroni in rapidly boiling salted water according to package directions; drain.

Heat tomatoes with juice; add to macaroni, along with salt and pepper to taste, stirring well to combine. Add a splash of tomato juice or V-8 if mixture is too dry. Serves 4.

Cook's note: If desired, stir in 1 tablespoon thinly sliced fresh basil leaves and 1 tablespoon chopped fresh oregano and top with freshly grated parmesan cheese just before serving.

SAY CHEESE

That childhood favorite macaroni and cheese has experienced something of a renaissance recently. No longer relegated to cafeterias and kiddie menus, mac and cheese has gained an adult sensibility, appearing at upscale restaurants paired with such gourmet ingredients as lobster or pancetta.

Chefs call it grown-up comfort food and find that the basic combo of pasta in cheese sauce can easily be dressed up—or down—as desired. It's a popular side dish at main street cafes and other casual restaurants, and you'll even spot it at drive-ins, sliced into wedges, breaded and deep-fried.

Basic macaroni and cheese recipes can go from everyday to gourmet with the addition of such ingredients as sautéed onions or leeks, crumbled bacon, dry mustard, or a pinch of nutmeg. Or go for a bolder flavor by using extra-sharp cheddar and Parmigiano-Reggiano cheese instead of the regular variety.

For a sophisticated presentation, bake it in individual ramekins, adding a buttery breadcrumb topping for those who prefer it and leaving some plain for the mac and cheese purists at the dinner table. —J.K.

Baked Macaroni and Cheese

As much at home on the Friday dinner table as the Thanksgiving spread, macaroni and cheese is wholesomely Hoosier. But despite being an easy-to-prepare and popular side dish at Main Street cafes, no recipes came our way. This mac and cheese recipe, one of Jolene's favorites, lends itself well to additions.

        ¼ cup unsalted butter
        3 tablespoons flour
     2½ cups whole milk
        8 ounces (3 cups) coarsely grated cheddar
        ¼ cup grated parmesan
        1 teaspoon salt
        ¼ teaspoon pepper
        ½ pound elbow macaroni

Preheat oven to 400 degrees.

Melt butter in a heavy saucepan over medium-low heat; stir in flour and cook, stirring, for 1 to 2 minutes. Whisk in milk and bring to a boil, stirring constantly. Simmer, stirring occasionally for about 3 minutes. Stir in cheeses; add salt and pepper, stirring until smooth. Remove from heat and place waxed paper on top of sauce to prevent a skin from forming.

Cook macaroni in boiling, salted water until al dente. Reserve a cup of the cooking water and drain macaroni. Stir together macaroni and cheese sauce, adding some of the reserved water if sauce seems too thick. Place in a shallow 2-quart baking dish and bake until bubbly, about 20 minutes. Serves 8.

Cook's note: For an optional topping to sprinkle on before baking, stir together 2 tablespoons melted butter with 1 cup breadcrumbs, ¾ cup coarsely grated cheddar, and ¼ cup grated parmesan cheese.

SIX

~ ~ ~

Pies

PIE CRUST

Pie remains the quintessential cafe dessert. Whether you make it from scratch or just pour canned filling into a store-bought crust, there's something comforting about fresh-baked pie.

Indiana cafes commonly use frozen pie crusts (Wick's pie crusts, made in Winchester, are a popular option) and packaged graham cracker crusts. They certainly deliver a tasty pie, and customers clamor for a slice of just-baked goodness—made even better with a scoop of ice cream.

But for a real cafe-inspired treat, take the time to make a homemade pie crust—then fill it with peaches, rhubarb, coconut pudding, or sugar cream for a real slice of Indiana.

The key to a tender, flaky pie crust is ice water and chilled butter or shortening. Some folks swear by lard, others by butter-flavored shortening. Whichever type you use, do keep it chilled.

(continued on facing page)

Pastry for Two-Crust Pie

While many cafe owners rely on the convenient, Indiana-made Wick's frozen pie crusts, homemade crusts certainly appeal, and we couldn't resist including a couple of favorite scratch recipes. Here's Jolene's favorite pie crust recipe, based on one found in *Joy of Cooking* by Irma S. Rombauer, Marion Rombauer Becker, and Ethan Becker. It's a classic.

$2\frac{1}{2}$ **cups flour**
  2   **teaspoons sugar**
  1   **teaspoon salt**
  6   **tablespoons cold butter**
 $\frac{1}{4}$ **cup vegetable shortening, chilled**
  6   **tablespoons ice water, plus an additional tablespoon, if necessary**

Sift together the flour, sugar, and salt. Cut the butter and one-half the shortening into the flour mixture until it is the consistency of cornmeal. Cut in the rest of the shortening until the mixture resembles pea-size clumps.

Sprinkle flour mixture with 6 tablespoons ice water, stirring with a fork until it just holds together. If necessary, add water, 1 teaspoon at a time.

Divide dough in half, shape into disks, and wrap each in plastic wrap. Refrigerate at least 30 minutes but no longer than 12 hours. Before using, allow dough to stand at room temperature just until it becomes pliable. Roll out as needed. Makes one 9-inch double-crust pie.

Never-Fail Pie Crust

Joanne's favorite pie crust recipe is adapted from one in *Heartland: The Best of the Old and the New from Midwest Kitchens* by Marcia Adams. The dough can be kept in the freezer and thawed whenever the mood to make pie strikes.

$4\frac{1}{4}$ **cups unbleached flour**
  1   **teaspoon baking powder**
  2   **teaspoons salt**
  1   **teaspoon sugar**

½ **cup ice water**
1 **egg**
1 **teaspoon cider vinegar**
1¾ **cups butter-flavored Crisco**
1 **tablespoon milk**
    additional sugar for sprinkling

(continued from facing page)

In a medium bowl, whisk together flour, baking powder, salt, and sugar. Set aside.

Measure out water and put in freezer to chill. In a small bowl, beat together the egg and vinegar. Set aside.

In a large bowl, beat the Crisco with an electric mixer at medium speed until creamy. At low speed, add the flour mixture by spoonfuls, mixing thoroughly. Scrape down the beaters with a table knife as necessary.

Remove the water from the freezer and add it to the egg and vinegar mixture, stirring well. At medium speed, add this mixture slowly in a pencil-size stream to the flour mixture, scraping down the sides of the bowl with a rubber spatula. When the mixture holds together, turn it out onto a surface and knead by hand for about 45 seconds, or until shortening is thoroughly mixed into the dough.

Divide the dough into 4 to 6 rounds and put each one in a resealable plastic sandwich bag. Put the bags in the freezer. No more than 8 hours before you want to make a pie, thaw a round of dough (2 rounds for a double-crust pie) in the refrigerator. The dough will darken and get sour if it's kept in the refrigerator more than 48 hours. Do not thaw it at room temperature because the dough must be cold when it's rolled out.

For pies that require a baked shell, lay the rolled crust into a pan and prick it all over with a fork. Bake at 425 degrees for about 10 to 15 minutes. Check it often so it does not get darker than you like. Cool before filling.

For two-crust pies that are to be baked in the oven, lay rolled out dough into a pan, add the filling, and set aside. Roll out the top crust and lay it on top of the filling, crimping the edges to seal them. Using a knife, cut a few slits into the top crust to allow steam to escape. Brush or gently rub milk onto the top crust and sprinkle with sugar. Bake according to individual recipe instructions. Makes 4 to 6 single crusts.

Don't overmix the dough; you want to see pieces of the butter or shortening, pieces that will melt during baking to create the much-coveted flaky crust. To ensure a tender crust, chill the dough for at least a half hour before rolling it out, and handle it as little as possible.

You'll find a few from-scratch pie crusts in Indiana cafes, and when you do, savor every bite. Or even better, order a whole pie ahead of time to take home. —J.K.

Buttermilk Pie

PALMER HOUSE, BERNE

Sharon and Roger LeFever and Saundra and Keith Minger

Rich with butter and eggs, this old-fashioned favorite satisfies, even with a slim slice. A fondness for buttermilk is just one clue to the Appalachian heritage of many Hoosier foods (see sidebar on page 104). Traditionally, buttermilk is the liquid that remains after milk is churned into butter. Today, however, it is commercially cultured.

2½ **cups sugar**
¼ **cup flour**
1 **cup butter or margarine, melted**
6 **eggs, beaten**
1⅓ **cups buttermilk**
1 **teaspoon lemon zest**
1 **9-inch pie shell, unbaked**

Stir together sugar and flour in a large mixing bowl. Add melted butter or margarine, eggs, buttermilk, and lemon zest, mixing well to combine. Pour into unbaked pie shell and bake at 350 degrees for 35 to 45 minutes. Serves 6 to 8.

Custard Pie

PALMER HOUSE, BERNE
Sharon and Roger LeFever and Saundra and Keith Minger

Simple ingredients create a tasty dessert with this rich, sweet recipe. Add a sprinkle of nutmeg along with the cinnamon.

- **1 cup milk**
- **1 cup half-and-half**
- **3 eggs, beaten**
- **¾ cup sugar**
- **pinch salt**
- **1 tablespoon cornstarch**
- **1 teaspoon vanilla extract**
- **1 9-inch pie shell, unbaked**
- **cinnamon**

Heat milk and half-and-half in a medium saucepan over medium-low heat. Whisk in eggs.

In a small bowl, whisk together sugar, salt, and cornstarch. Add to milk mixture, stirring well until sugar dissolves. Bring to a simmer, stirring, until mixture starts to thicken. Remove from heat and stir in vanilla. Pour into pie shell and sprinkle with cinnamon. Bake at 375 degrees about 25 to 30 minutes. Serves 6.

Rhubarb Custard Pie

PALMER HOUSE, BERNE

Sharon and Roger LeFever and Saundra and Keith Minger

Get sweet on typically tart rhubarb with this variation on the classic custard pie.

- 1¼ cup granulated sugar
- 1 tablespoon flour
- pinch salt
- 2 eggs, beaten
- 1¾ cup half-and-half
- 1 teaspoon vanilla extract
- 2 cups chopped rhubarb (thawed, drained, and squeezed dry, if necessary)
- pastry for double-crust pie

Whisk together sugar, flour, and salt in a medium bowl. Add eggs, half-and-half, and vanilla, mixing well to combine.

Stir rhubarb into sugar mixture. Line pie pan with crust. Pour in filling. Cover with top crust and crimp edges decoratively. Bake at 375 degrees for 45 minutes to an hour. Serves 6.

Rhubarb Pie 🏴

Rhubarb is a harbinger of spring in Indiana, and the bright red stalks of "pie plant" are an early garden favorite, especially when baked into recipes like this one. Based on the number of times Joanne encountered rhubarb pie—and ate it, too!—during her two-year cafe adventure, rhubarb is a close second to coconut cream for the title of favorite Hoosier pie. We offer this as a representative of all those recipes cherished but not contributed by cafe owners.

- 1⅓ cups sugar
- 6 tablespoons flour
- 4 cups chopped rhubarb
- 2 tablespoons butter
- pastry for 9-inch double-crust pie
- 1 tablespoon milk
- additional sugar for sprinkling

Preheat oven to 450 degrees. Arrange bottom crust in 9-inch pie pan. Stir together sugar and flour. Sprinkle ⅓ cup of sugar and flour mixture over bottom crust. Add rhubarb. Sprinkle with remaining sugar and flour mixture. Dot with butter. Cover with top crust and crimp edges. Brush top crust with milk; sprinkle with sugar. Cut several small vents in top crust. Place pie on lowest oven rack and bake for 15 minutes. Reduce temperature to 350 degrees and bake for 40 to 45 more minutes. Serve warm with vanilla ice cream, if desired. Serves 8.

Cook's note: When strawberries ripen in June, replace 2 cups of the rhubarb with 2 cups of fresh sliced berries for another Hoosier classic: strawberry-rhubarb pie.

Baked Coconut Pie

PALMER HOUSE, BERNE
Sharon and Roger LeFever and Saundra and Keith Minger

A favorite of Keith's mother, this pretty pie bakes up with a lacy, light-brown top. Palmer House regulars know it makes a sweet finale to any meal.

- ½ cup butter
- 2 eggs, beaten
- 1 teaspoon salt
- 1½ cups sugar
- ¼ cup flour
- ¾ cup milk
- 1¾ cups shredded coconut
- 1 teaspoon vanilla extract
- 1 9-inch pie shell, unbaked

In a medium saucepan, melt butter over medium heat. Stir in eggs. In a small bowl, whisk together salt, sugar, and flour. Add dry mixture to butter and egg mixture, stirring well to combine. Cook, stirring, until mixture simmers and thickens slightly. Stir in milk and coconut. Remove from heat and stir in vanilla. Pour into unbaked pie shell and bake at 375 degrees about 35 minutes until lightly browned. Serves 6.

Coconut Pie ★

WINDELL'S CAFE, DALE
Darrel and Betty Jenkins

Based on the comments of cafe owners and customers and its prevalence on daily specials boards, coconut cream is the most popular pie in Hoosier cafes. This recipe was handed down from Bob and Margaret Windell, who opened the cafe in 1947. The pie was featured in *Midwest Living* magazine in June 1994.

> 5 **eggs, separated**
> 1 **cup plus 1 tablespoon sugar**
> 2 **cups milk**
> 1 **teaspoon vanilla extract**
> 3½ **tablespoons cornstarch**
> ⅓ **cup shredded coconut, plus more for sprinkling**
> 1 **9-inch pie shell, baked**

Combine egg yolks, 1 cup sugar, milk, vanilla, and cornstarch in a 1-quart saucepan. Cook over medium heat, stirring constantly, until thickened. Remove from heat and stir in ⅓ cup coconut. Pour mixture into baked pie shell; set aside.

   With an electric mixer, beat egg whites at medium speed until stiff peaks form. Add 1 tablespoon sugar and beat another 30 seconds. Arrange meringue on pie and sprinkle with coconut. Bake at 350 degrees until golden brown. Allow to cool 30 minutes before serving. Serves 6 to 8.

SUGAR CREAM PIE—A SWEET SLICE OF INDIANA HISTORY

Hoosier schoolchildren study Indiana history in the fourth grade, duly memorizing key dates and events, as well as such details as the state's official flower (the peony) and bird (the cardinal). But now students have a bit of tasty trivia to commit to memory. In 2009, the Indiana legislature recommended sugar cream pie as the state's official pie.

While some around the state may be unfamiliar with the recipe—a simple combination of sugar, flour, cream, vanilla, and nutmeg—it has long been a farmhouse favorite. Made with pantry staples, the sugar cream pie was likely a common winter treat made when fruit was unavailable. According to the Indiana Foodways Alliance (IFA), an association focused on the development and promotion of Indiana's food culture, the Hoosier sugar cream pie originated in eastern Indiana Quaker settlements between 1810 and 1825. Other food historians attribute its origins to Dutch and German immigrants moving into the Hoosier state from Pennsylvania, the Indiana Shaker community of the early nineteenth century, and migrants from Appalachia who brought "transparent pie" with them.

You'll find authentic Hoosier sugar cream pie in almost every small-town cafe throughout the state, including Storie's Restaurant in Greensburg, which gets a callout on the IFA Web site. But the sugar cream pie capital of Indiana is clearly Winchester, where Wick's Pies produces more than 750,000 of them each year.

All that pie production prompted Indiana Senator Allen Paul of nearby Richmond to sponsor the resolution, researched and backed by IFA, recommending that sugar cream be known as Hoosier Pie and be officially recognized as the state pie.

While Wick's produces twelve million pies and pie shells each year for the baking and food service industry, as well as for retail sales, the company says it remains best known for its old-fashioned sugar cream pie.

"Traditionally an Indiana product," notes the company's Web site, "Wick's Sugar Cream Pie is produced from a Wickersham family recipe that dates back to the nineteenth-century farm."

Mike Wickersham, son of company founder Duane "Wick" Wickersham, was on hand at the Indiana Statehouse—handing out slices of sugar cream pie, of course—when the legislature recommended that sugar cream be designated Indiana's state pie.

"It's a great honor," Wickersham told the *Indianapolis Star.* "The sugar cream pie is a great pie, and it's a Hoosier pie. Every state needs a state pie."—J.K.

TASTY TRAVEL ALONG INDIANA'S CULINARY TRAILS

Joanne traversed the state to find Indiana's best small-town restaurants, and the result was *Cafe Indiana: A Guide to Indiana's Down-Home Cafes.* That led to this cookbook, which allows you to re-create some of the favorite dishes from those cafes.

But what if you want more? What if you want to spend a day, a weekend, or even longer exploring the state and sampling the great variety of real, good food Indiana has to offer?

Well, you won't be alone.

Studies show that nearly two-thirds of American vacationers are interested in culinary travel. In fact, sixteen million Americans say that they plan their vacations around food.

And why not? Especially in Indiana, there are all sorts of food destinations worth a visit. In addition to the great

(continued on facing page)

Old-Fashioned Cream Pie

PALMER HOUSE, BERNE
Sharon and Roger LeFever and Saundra and Keith Minger

There are many ways to make Hoosier classic sugar cream pie. This baked recipe combines white and brown sugar with thick cream to create a pie that is smooth, rich, and sweet. Simplicity lends itself to many variations, such as the two recipes that follow.

- ¾ cup brown sugar
- ¾ cup white sugar
- ¾ cup flour
- ½ teaspoon cinnamon
- pinch salt
- 1⅔ cups heavy whipping cream
- 1½ cups half-and-half
- 1 teaspoon vanilla extract
- 1 9-inch pie shell, unbaked

In a large bowl, whisk together sugars, flour, cinnamon, and salt. Add heavy whipping cream, half-and-half, and vanilla, stirring well to combine. Pour into pie shell. Sprinkle with additional cinnamon. Bake at 375 degrees for 40 to 45 minutes. Serves 6.

Sugar Cream Pie #1

NEWBERRY CAFE, NEWBERRY
Lois and Lanny Pickett

Although sugar cream pie has been recommended by the legislature as the official state pie of Indiana (see sidebar), Lois says many customers have never head of it. That doesn't keep them from trying it, though. "I serve this once a week," she says. "It goes real fast." Lois prepares the rich filling on the stovetop, pours it into the baked crust, and then slides the pie into the oven to set and brown.

- 1 cup sugar
- scant ½ cup cornstarch
- 2 cups half-and-half
- ½ cup margarine

(continued from facing page)

1 teaspoon vanilla extract
1 9-inch pie shell
   nutmeg and cinnamon

Combine sugar and cornstarch in a medium saucepan. Slowly add half-and-half and cook over medium-high heat, stirring, just until mixture simmers and thickens. Add margarine and vanilla, stirring until margarine melts. Pour filling into baked pie shell. Sprinkle with nutmeg and cinnamon. Bake at 325 degrees for 15 to 20 minutes. Serves 6.

Sugar Cream Pie #2

Bobbie Jo's Diner, Edinburgh
Bobbie Jo Hart

Cook Bertha Burton has been making this rich, sweet dessert for years. As with the recipe above, this recipe has the filling cooked on the stovetop before being poured into a baked pie shell. It then sets up without additional time in the oven. "This is so easy, and it's so good," says Bertha, although she does offer a bit of advice: "Keep stirring. Don't stop stirring."

½ cup sugar
¼ cup cornstarch
1 (12-ounce) can Milnot evaporated milk
½ cup water
1 teaspoon vanilla extract
½ cup butter
¼ teaspoon cinnamon
1 9-inch pie shell, baked

Combine sugar and cornstarch in a small bowl. Heat milk and water in a medium saucepan. Add vanilla, butter, and cinnamon and bring mixture nearly to a boil. Stir in sugar and cornstarch mixture, a little at a time, stirring constantly. Cook, stirring constantly, over medium-low heat until mixture thickens. Quickly pour into baked pie shell. Dust with cinnamon. Serves 6.

restaurants profiled in *Cafe Indiana*, you can find plenty of delicious reasons to travel around the state, courtesy of the Indiana Foodways Alliance (IFA). Members of the I-69 Cultural Corridor Association founded the IFA in 2007 after commissioning a study that turned up nearly seventy rural culinary tourism sites in northeastern Indiana alone.

That led to the identification of other unique food destinations around the state and the development of the IFA's culinary trails. Spotlighting everything from tearooms to tenderloins, the trails lead visitors from one food-related destination to another.

Some, such as the Hoosier Pie Trail, include venues around the state. Others zero in on specific regions. But wherever the trails lead, you're sure to find something tasty along the way. For more info, go to www.indianafoodways.com. —J.K.

Pie Palooza

Thinking I'd beat the rush, I arrived at the Palmer House for the famed Friday night buffet at the opening hour of 4 p.m. I was a solo diner until members of the Wally Byam Caravan Club showed up at about five. Senior citizens all, the campers had been led to Berne's family restaurant by an advance scout, who asked several times about the Palmer House's ability to seat and serve the large group. Twice he asked for confirmation about the price per person, which is an unbelievable bargain. The price includes a salad and hot food bar, plus a dessert bar to die for.

Only shame at my gluttony, so cruelly exposed to the entire Caravan Club, keeps me from taking some of everything. Stretched out before me is a dreamlike candyland, a veritable feast of sweets: thick butterscotch pudding, a layered spice cake with vanilla icing, fudge

(continued on facing page)

Peach Cream Pie

Palmer House, Berne

Sharon and Roger LeFever and Saundra and Keith Minger

This is the top-seller of more than two dozen varieties of Palmer House pie. Kick it up a notch in the summer by substituting fresh, tree-ripened peaches.

- ¾ cup sugar
- 2 heaping tablespoons flour
- pinch salt
- 1 (29-ounce) can sliced peaches, drained
- 1¾ cup heavy whipping cream
- pastry for 9-inch double-crust pie
- cinnamon

In a large bowl, whisk together sugar, flour, and salt. Add peaches, stirring to combine. Stir in whipping cream.

Line pie pan with crust. Add peach mixture, sprinkle with cinnamon, and cover with top crust, crimping edges decoratively. Bake at 375 degrees about 1 hour or until crust is lightly browned. Serves 6.

Apple Cream Pie

PALMER HOUSE, BERNE
Sharon and Roger LeFever and Saundra and Keith Minger

Imagine à la mode baked directly into an apple pie.

- ½ **cup brown sugar**
- ½ **cup granulated sugar**
- 1 **heaping tablespoon flour**
- 1 **cup whipping cream**
- 2 **cups peeled, cored, and sliced tart apples, such as Granny Smith (2 to 3 large apples)**
- **pastry for double-crust pie**
- **cinnamon**

In a large bowl, whisk together sugars and flour. Add whipping cream, mixing well to combine. Stir in apples.

Line pie pan with crust. Add apple mixture, sprinkle with cinnamon, and cover with top crust, crimping edges decoratively. Bake at 375 degrees about 1 hour or until crust is lightly browned. Serves 6.

Apple Butter Pie

PALMER HOUSE, BERNE
Sharon and Roger LeFever and Saundra and Keith Minger

Enjoy the autumn flavor of this old-fashioned pie with a scoop of vanilla ice cream. For an apple butter recipe used for more than thirty years at Chambers Smorgasbord in Spencer, see page 98.

- ½ **cup sugar**
- 1 **heaping tablespoon flour**
- 5 **tablespoons apple butter**
- 2 **eggs, beaten**
- 1¾ **cup milk**
- 1 **(8-inch) pie shell, unbaked**

Preheat oven to 425 degrees. In a mixing bowl, combine sugar and flour. Add apple butter, eggs, and milk; mix well. Pour into pie shell and bake for 10 minutes. Reduce heat to 350 degrees and bake for 30 to 35 more minutes or until knife inserted in middle comes out clean. Serves 6.

(continued from facing page)

brownies, and pie, pie, pie. A three-tiered, stair-stepped display shelf holds tempting triangles laid out on ceramic plates like gems in a jeweler's case. Apricot, lattice-topped raspberry, old-fashioned cream pie, peach cream, rhubarb custard, chocolate, dutch apple. Mercy! How can I possibly choose?

Keith Minger directs me toward the peach cream (the top seller of twenty-three varieties of Palmer House pie) and the baked coconut, his mother's favorite. Just one bite of each substantiates a fundamental principle of adventure-eating: anything out of the ordinary is bound to be good.

With a kind of deflating sadness and not just a little discomfort, I say good-bye to Keith and his wife, Saundra, and the Palmer House. Before I leave Main Street for the highway, I am already thinking of my next visit to Berne. I can't wait. —J.S., adapted from *Cafe Indiana*

Raisin Pie

GOSPORT DINER, GOSPORT
Floyd and Donna Friend

This old-fashioned pie—both economical and easy—is still favored by some of Donna's customers, so she tried her best to recreate her mother's classic recipe. "No one could make a raisin pie like my mom," says Donna. "This is the closest thing to her raisin pie as I can come."

>**pastry for 10-inch deep-dish double-crust pie**
>**4 cups raisins**
>**1⅓ cups brown sugar**
>**scant ½ cup cornstarch**
>**⅛ teaspoon salt**
>**1 cup orange juice**
>**½ cup lemon juice**
>**2 cups water**
>**3 tablespoons butter**
>**1 egg white, beaten**
>**granulated sugar for sprinkling**

Preheat oven to 375 degrees. Arrange bottom crust in 10-inch deep-dish pie pan.

Place raisins in heavy saucepan. Stir together brown sugar, cornstarch, and salt; sprinkle over raisins, stirring well to combine. Add orange juice and lemon juice and heat over medium heat, stirring until sugar is dissolved. Add water and cook, stirring, until mixture is thickened and deep brown in color.

Pour into prepared pie pan; dot with butter. Cover with top crust and crimp edges. Brush top crust with beaten egg white; sprinkle with sugar. Cut several slits in top crust; bake for 45 minutes until crust is browned and filling is bubbly. Serves 8.

Cook's note: For apple-raisin pie, omit 1 cup of raisins and add 1 cup diced apple, 1 teaspoon cinnamon, and ½ teaspoon nutmeg.

COOKING WITHOUT RECIPES

At the Gosport Diner, Donna and Floyd Friend's customers often ask for recipes, so often, in fact, that Donna has contemplated writing a cookbook when she and Floyd retire "at the end of all this." When our request for favorite cafe recipes turned up in their mailbox, the issue came up once again.

"I asked myself, 'How would I do it?'" Donna says. How would she translate into words the intuition, rhythm, and habit of many years of cooking without recipes? The feel of good biscuit dough between her fingers? The look of cream pie filling that needs more milk? The quantity of ground beef in the bowl that Floyd always uses to make meat loaf?

"I have very few recipes that are written down. Most of my or our recipes are some of this, a dash of that, this looks good, smells good, or I'd eat it so it's good. Someday I may get in the kitchen and measure out our dashes, pinches, and squirts and put it to paper. [She did just that for the raisin pie recipe included here.] I've thought about writing a cookbook just like that. I think another cook would know just what I mean."

Ironically, for one who professes a dislike for cooking—"I never really have [liked to cook], I know it's a strange thing"—Donna is blessed with an instinctual gift. Like a musician who picks out a tune on the keyboard after hearing it once, Donna looks at a dish and knows just how to make it. She "finagles" with ingredients, tweaking and personalizing sometimes for a month or more, until taste, texture, and appearance are "just right."

She does the same with recipes, which she regards with suspended faith if not downright distrust. Time and again, promising dishes turn into flops because people make mistakes when they write things down.

"I got an oatmeal pie recipe from a restaurant in Indianapolis," she says. "I could tell it would not work, but I went ahead and made it, and it didn't work. It didn't set up. The eggs were left out. It baked for only thirty minutes, and that wasn't right either.

"If I find a recipe I might like, I never make it the way it is written. I always add extra of what I like, delete what I don't like, and do a lot of substituting. Doing this makes it my creation."—J.S.

Sugar-Free Strawberry Pie

VICKY'S RESTAURANT, WINAMAC
Vicky and David Pingel

Vicky created this recipe in response to customers' requests for sugar-free fruit desserts. "This pie goes like crazy in the summer," she says. "My customers rave about it."

>   1 **cup Splenda**
>   2 **tablespoons cornstarch**
> 1 ½ **cups cold water**
>   1 **(4-ounce) box sugar-free strawberry-flavored gelatin**
>   2 **quarts strawberries, hulled and sliced**
>   1 **(9-inch) pie shell, baked**

In a medium saucepan, stir together Splenda and cornstarch; add water. Cook, stirring, over medium heat until mixture simmers and thickens. Remove from heat and add gelatin, stirring well to combine. Cool; refrigerate until chilled and thickened, at least an hour.

Add strawberries to gelatin mixture. Pour into cooled, baked pie shell. Refrigerate at least an hour before serving. Serves 6 to 8.

Quick as a Wink Pie

BOBBIE JO'S DINER, EDINBURGH
Bobbie Jo Hart

This cool confection is the best-selling pie at Bobbie Jo's Diner, made by cook Bertha Burton for many years from a recipe she got from her sister. "We have it often but not all the time because it is so rich," she says. "You can substitute canned or fresh peaches, raspberries, strawberries, blackberries, or any other kind of fruit for the pineapple."

>   1 **(15-ounce) can crushed pineapple, undrained**
>   1 **(4-ounce) box vanilla instant pudding**
>   1 **(8-ounce) package Philadelphia cream cheese, softened**
>   1 **(8-ounce) tub frozen nondairy whipped topping, thawed**
>   1 **9-inch graham cracker pie crust or baked pastry shell**

In a large bowl, combine pineapple and dry pudding mix. Using a spoon, stir in cream cheese until mixture is smooth. Stir in half of the whipped topping. Pour mixture into pie shell. Cover and refrigerate until ready to serve. Serves 6 to 8.

Peanut Butter Pie

VELMA'S DINER, SHOALS
Debbie Montgomery

A variation of this classic frozen pie is often served at Velma's Diner, where Debbie serves it drizzled with chocolate syrup and sprinkled with peanut butter chips.

- 1 (3-ounce) package cream cheese, softened
- 1 cup powdered sugar
- ½ cup creamy peanut butter
- ½ cup milk
- 1 (8-ounce) tub frozen nondairy whipped topping, thawed
- 1 9-inch graham cracker pie crust
  chocolate syrup and peanut butter chips (optional)

In a large mixing bowl, beat cream cheese with an electric mixer on low speed until fluffy; slowly add sugar. Beat in peanut butter on medium speed until well mixed. Slowly beat in milk. By hand, fold in whipped topping. Pour into pie crust. Drizzle with chocolate syrup and garnish with peanut butter chips, if desired. Freeze several hours before serving. Makes 1 pie.

Maw Maw's Pie

BABY BOOMERS CAFE, HAMILTON
Penny Hawkins

Penny occasionally offers complimentary slices of this family favorite to customers; once they've tasted a rich, sweet slice, they sometimes buy a whole pie. "It is so good, it should be outlawed," she says.

- ½ cup butter
- 1 (7-ounce) bag shredded coconut
- ½ cup chopped pecans
- 1 (8-ounce) package cream cheese, softened
- 1 (8-ounce) tub frozen nondairy whipped topping, thawed
- 1 (14-ounce) can sweetened condensed milk
- 2 9-inch graham cracker pie crusts
- ½ cup caramel topping

In a nonstick skillet or medium saucepan, melt butter over medium-low heat. Add coconut and pecans and stir, cooking until coconut browns and pecans are toasted, 1 to 2 minutes. Set aside to cool.

In a medium bowl, mix cream cheese, whipped topping, and condensed milk. Pour a layer of cream cheese mixture into each pie shell. Add a layer of coconut mixture and another layer of the cream cheese mixture, ending with coconut. Drizzle each pie with about ¼ cup caramel topping. Freeze for several hours; keep in freezer until ready to serve. Serves 6 to 8.

SEVEN

~ ~ ~

Desserts

Peanut Butter No-Bake Cookies

CHAMBERS SMORGASBORD, SPENCER

Barbara Chambers and Jim Chambers

Barbara says her late husband, Bob, thought there were too many chocolate desserts on the buffet, so he came up with this one. "Peanut Butter No-Bake Cookies are probably one of our customers' most asked-for desserts," she says. "They are often called our peanut butter fudge."

  ¹/₂ **cup butter**
   1 **cup milk**
   3 **cups sugar**
   1 **(20-ounce) jar peanut butter**
   4 **cups quick-cooking oats**
   1 **teaspoon vanilla extract**

In a large, heavy saucepan, melt butter with milk and sugar over medium heat. Bring to a boil and cook, stirring for 1 minute. Remove from heat. Stir in peanut butter, oats, and vanilla; mix well.

Spray 9-by-13-inch baking pan with cooking spray. Spread mixture into prepared pan. Let cool completely and cut into squares. Makes 24 squares.

"Reese's" Peanut Butter Candy

CHAMBERS SMORGASBORD, SPENCER

Barbara Chambers and Jim Chambers

Barbara says this treat—reminiscent of the popular chocolate-covered peanut butter cups—has been served at the restaurant for the past thirty years. "Reese's are only served on Sunday," she says, "with our special Sunday buffet."

 1¹/₂ **cups butter, divided**
   1 **(40-ounce) jar peanut butter**
   1 **cup instant dry milk powder**
   4 **cups powdered sugar**
   3 **tablespoons vanilla extract, divided**
  ²/₃ **cup hot water**
   3 **cups granulated sugar**

²⁄₃ **cup evaporated milk**
1 **cup semisweet chocolate chips**

Melt ½ cup (1 stick) butter. In a large mixing bowl, combine melted butter, peanut butter, dry milk, powdered sugar, 2 tablespoons vanilla, and hot water. Spray 11-by-17-inch pan with cooking spray. Pour mixture into prepared pan.

In a medium saucepan over medium heat, melt the remaining 1 cup (2 sticks) butter; add the granulated sugar and evaporated milk, stirring well. Bring to a boil and cook, stirring, for 2 minutes. Remove from heat; add the remaining tablespoon vanilla and chocolate chips, whisking until chips are melted. Pour over peanut butter mixture in pan, spreading with spoon. Chill, then cut into small squares. Makes 48 pieces.

Lemon Bar Deluxe

Baby Boomers Cafe, Hamilton
Penny Hawkins

This treat comes from Penny's family's cookbook, a collection of their own favorite recipes. The bars can also be made with orange or pineapple juice instead of lemon.

2¼ **cups flour, divided**
 ½ **cup powdered sugar**
 1 **cup butter, softened**
 4 **eggs, beaten**
 2 **cups granulated sugar**
 ⅓ **cup lemon juice (from 2 lemons)**
 ½ **teaspoon baking powder**

For crust, mix together 2 cups flour, powdered sugar, and butter until well combined; pat into 9-by-13-inch pan. Bake at 350 degrees for 25 minutes.

For filling, combine eggs, granulated sugar, and lemon juice. Sift remaining ¼ cup flour and stir together with baking powder; add to egg mixture, stirring well to combine. Pour into baked crust. Bake at 350 degrees for 30 minutes. Cool and cut into squares; sprinkle with powdered sugar before serving. Makes 15 bars.

Brownies

CHAMBERS SMORGASBORD, SPENCER
Barbara Chambers and Jim Chambers

Barbara tried these brownies at a friend's house thirty years ago and had to have the recipe. Now they're popular at the restaurant too. "We serve the brownies almost daily on our buffet," she says. "They are very moist and fudgy and a favorite dessert with our customers."

- 1½ cups butter, divided
- 5 (1-ounce) squares Baker's unsweetened chocolate, divided
- 2 cups granulated sugar
- 2 cups flour
- 5 eggs, beaten
- 1 cup chopped walnuts
- 1 teaspoon vanilla extract
- 2 tablespoons milk
  confectioners' sugar

Melt 1¼ cups (2½ sticks) butter with 4 squares chocolate in a medium saucepan. Add granulated sugar, flour, eggs, walnuts, and vanilla. Stir with spoon until well mixed.

Spray a 9-by-13-inch baking pan with cooking spray; pour chocolate mixture into pan. Bake at 350 degrees for 25 to 30 minutes; do not overbake.

For frosting, melt remaining ¼ cup (½ stick) butter with remaining chocolate square; stir in milk. Add confectioners' sugar, a tablespoon at a time, until frosting is thick but still pourable.

When brownies are done, pour on frosting while still warm. Makes 24 squares.

Brownie Delight

OLD SCHOOL CAFE, PLEASANT
Roger and Dawn Christman

Judy May, head cook at the Old School Cafe, says everyone loves Brownie Delight, a so-easy dessert that is the restaurant's most popular. "Customers bring friends in to treat them to these," she says. Try it using the brownies made from the previous recipe.

> **3-by-4-inch brownie**
> 2 **scoops vanilla ice cream**
> **chocolate syrup**
> **whipped cream**

Top brownie with ice cream. Drizzle with chocolate syrup and garnish with whipped cream. Serves 1.

BACK TO SCHOOL

The Old School Cafe is just that: a former school housing grades one through eight that served Pleasant Township families from 1956 to 1981. Located next to the community park, ball field, and water tower, the red-brick school with a green metal roof has been converted into a kind of multiuse mini mall, with the cafe occupying the cafeteria, an apartment in two front classrooms, and a meat-processing business taking over the rear principal's office and sixth grade room. Out front you'll find a piece of vintage playground equipment, a covered front porch with a variety of outdoor tables and chairs, and potted caladiums.

Both inside and out, owner Roger Christman and his mom, Sue, have done little to disguise the fact that the building is a township school. Instead, they celebrate its history with school-themed antiques and collectibles, including the original green chalkboard in the cafeteria that serves as the daily specials board, old class photographs ("People love that," says Sue. "They like to see themselves when they were much younger."), and a cheer horn from the old Austin school, long since torn down. The main hall leading to the classrooms is filled with even more antiques, including a display of items related to tobacco farming, a restored Allis Chalmers tractor, and a pump organ. You'll find the cafe's rest rooms—the boys' and girls' lavatories—in the back hall as well. You can't mistake the boys'. On the door there's a picture of an outhouse with this caption: "Welcome to our Library and Music Room. Please remain seated during the entire performance."

Pleasant is a community in transition. Like most others of its size, Pleasant struggles to maintain its own cohesiveness and identity, especially since losing its school. The first change that marked the community's slow unraveling came in 1969 when the seventh- and eighth-grade students were bused to the high school in Vevay. A few years later, a change in the township districts took more of the Pleasant students out of the community, and in 1981, with the closing of the school, all of the students were sent elsewhere. "A lot of people were against consolidation, and the school had a very high rating as far as academics," Sue remembers.

With all Switzerland County students now centralized in two elementary schools and the middle school–high school campus at Vevay, the Pleasant Township School remains just one of three still standing in the county. Joy Briggs, a retired teacher, notes with sadness the loss of the school buildings that were once found scattered throughout the county. She cheers the rescue and reuse of the Pleasant Township School. "I think it's great. It would really be a shame to destroy it. All of our one-room schoolhouses are gone, and most of the township schools. When a community loses its school, it loses its identity."

More recently, Pleasant has lost other important community centers, like the old general store that yielded to the improvement and expansion of Indiana 129. Since then, "the restaurant has become the only place for people to gather," says Sue. "We have a lot of men who come here every day—some several times a day. They talk and talk and talk. For some, we're probably the only connection to the community that they have." —J.S., adapted from *Cafe Indiana*

Texas Sheet Cake

Vicky's Restaurant, Winamac
Vicky and David Pingel

Vicky offers this moist cake as a side dish option every Wednesday. "It is one of our most popular sides," she says, "and usually the whole pan is gone before lunch is done."

Sheet Cake
- 1 **cup flour**
- 1 **cup sugar**
- 1 **teaspoon baking soda**
- 1 **teaspoon cinnamon**
- ½ **teaspoon salt**
- 2 **eggs**
- 1¼ **cup buttermilk**
- 1 **cup butter or margarine**
- 4 **heaping tablespoons cocoa**
- 1 **cup hot water**

Frosting
- 1 **(1-pound) box or bag confectioners' sugar**
- 1½ **cup chopped pecans**
- ¾ **cup butter or margarine**
- 4 **heaping tablespoons cocoa**
- 7 **tablespoons buttermilk**
- 1 **tablespoon vanilla extract**

For cake: Stir together first seven ingredients in a large mixing bowl.

Melt butter in a heavy saucepan over medium heat. Add cocoa, stirring well to mix. Add hot water and bring to a boil.

Add butter and cocoa mixture to ingredients in mixing bowl and stir together thoroughly. Pour onto greased rimmed cookie sheet. Bake at 350 degrees approximately 30 minutes.

For frosting: Place confectioners' sugar and pecans in mixing bowl. Melt butter in a small saucepan over medium heat. Stir in cocoa. Add buttermilk and bring to a boil. Remove from heat and stir in vanilla. Add to confectioners' sugar, stirring well to combine.

When sheet cake is done, remove from oven and immediately spread with hot frosting. Allow to cool before cutting. Makes about 30 small pieces.

Merry's Bread Pudding

BABY BOOMERS CAFE, HAMILTON
Penny Hawkins,

Penny credits a friend with providing this delicious bread pudding recipe, which is even better made with cinnamon raisin bread. "When I make it for Baby Boomers, I times the recipe by four," she says.

> **6 slices stale bread, broken into pieces (about 4 cups)**
> **2 cups milk**
> **2 eggs**
> **1 cup sugar**
> **½ teaspoon vanilla extract**
> **1 teaspoon cinnamon**
> **1 teaspoon salt**

Combine all ingredients in a large mixing bowl, stirring well to moisten bread. Spray 9-by-13-inch baking pan with cooking spray; pour bread mixture into pan. Bake at 350 degrees for 45 minutes to an hour or until golden brown. Serve with vanilla sauce (recipe follows). Serves 6.

> *Vanilla Sauce*
> **2 cups sugar**
> **1 tablespoon flour**
> **1 cup water**
> **½ cup butter**
> **½ cup evaporated milk**
> **1 teaspoon vanilla extract**

In a medium saucepan, stir together sugar and flour. Add water, butter, evaporated milk, and vanilla and cook over medium heat until sauce simmers and thickens slightly. Serve over bread pudding.

Peach Cobbler

OLD SCHOOL CAFE, PLEASANT
Roger and Dawn Christman

This is a classic example of a cake-style cobbler from Old School Cafe head cook Judy May. Fruit is spread in the bottom of a pan and the batter is poured over it, baking up beautifully with the fruit hidden beneath. While canned peaches may be used, thawed frozen peaches deliver better results. If you've got access to juicy fresh peaches, your version of this cobbler will be in a class by itself.

- 6 **cups sliced peaches**
- 2 **cups sugar, divided**
- 4 **cups buttermilk pancake mix**
- 3 **cups water**
- 2 **teaspoons vanilla extract**
- $\frac{1}{4}$ **teaspoon pumpkin pie spice or cinnamon (optional)**
  melted butter (optional)

Preheat oven to 350 degrees. Butter a 9-by-13-inch baking dish.

In a large bowl, combine peaches and $1\frac{1}{2}$ cups of the sugar; place in baking dish. In a medium bowl, stir together pancake mix and water; stir in vanilla, the remaining $\frac{1}{2}$ cup sugar, and the pumpkin pie spice or cinnamon, if using. Pour mixture over the fruit. Bake for 1 hour to 1 hour 15 minutes, until deep golden brown. Top with melted butter, if desired. Serves 10.

Fruit Cobbler #1

Wolcott Theatre Cafe, Wolcott
Ann Cain

Ann calls this versatile recipe, used by her family for decades, "the gold standard for your basic cobbler." She suggests trying different combinations of fruit and flavoring: cherries, blueberries, or peaches with almond extract; apples, pears, or rhubarb with maple extract.

> 2 tablespoons vegetable shortening
> 1½ cups sugar, divided
> 1 cup flour
> 1 teaspoon baking powder
> ½ cup milk
>   pinch salt
> 2 cups fresh fruit, or 1 quart canned fruit with ¼ cup juice
> 2 cups water
> ¼ cup butter
> ½ teaspoon cinnamon
> ½ teaspoon vanilla extract

Preheat oven to 350 degrees. In a mixing bowl, combine shortening, ½ cup sugar, flour, baking powder, milk, and salt. Spray an 8-inch-square baking pan with cooking spray and spread the mixture in the pan.

In a medium saucepan, heat the rest of the ingredients, including the remaining cup of sugar. Pour over batter in pan. Bake for approximately 30 minutes. Serve warm, with a drizzle of heavy cream or a scoop of ice cream, if desired. Serves 8.

Fruit Cobbler #2

BOBBIE JO'S DINER, EDINBURGH
Bobbie Jo Hart

The cobblers served at Indiana cafes come in many varieties. Some have one crust, some have two. Like the two above, some are cakey, while others are more like pie. This recipe for a double-crust cobbler from beloved cook Bertha Burton puts it into the pie-like category. The type of fruit to use is up to you. Blackberry, peach, apple—it's all good, and even better with a scoop of ice cream.

4 to 6 cups fresh fruit or frozen, thawed
 ¹⁄₂ cup sugar
 1 teaspoon apple pie spice
 2 tablespoons cornstarch
 ¹⁄₂ cup water
    pastry for double-crust pie
 2 tablespoons butter, melted

Preheat oven to 350 degrees. In a heavy saucepan, stir together fruit and sugar, adjusting amount of sugar to taste; stir in apple pie spice. Bring to a simmer over medium heat, stirring until sugar is dissolved.

In a small bowl, combine cornstarch and water, stirring well. Slowly add to fruit mixture, stirring constantly until mixture thickens. Remove from heat and set aside.

On a floured surface, roll dough for bottom crust to fit 9-by-13-inch baking pan. Place crust in bottom of pan. Roll dough for top crust into similar size.

Place fruit in pan; cover with top crust. Brush top crust with melted butter and bake until crust is browned and filling is bubbly, about 45 minutes. Serves 10.

Cook's note: If using peaches, add ¹⁄₂ teaspoon cinnamon (or to taste) to fruit mixture.

Hummel Fummel

PALMER HOUSE, BERNE

Sharon and Roger LeFever and Saundra and Keith Minger

The name of this Swiss Mennonite treat is lost in translation. It appears to roughly correlate with *Himmel Frucht*—German for "heaven" or "sky" fruit—perhaps because of the fluffy cloud of whipped cream. Over forty years ago, then-owner Gaylord Stuckey made it part of the Friday night smorgasbord. "He was proud of the dessert and people really liked it, if they liked dates," says Saundra. "It was unique to the Palmer House, and he didn't give out the recipe."

2 eggs, beaten
1 cup sugar
2 heaping tablespoons flour
1 cup chopped dates
1 cup chopped pecans
2 bananas, sliced
2 (14-ounce) cans mandarin oranges, drained
1 (8-ounce) tub frozen nondairy whipped topping, thawed

Spray 9-by-13-inch baking pan with cooking spray.

Combine eggs, sugar, and flour in a large mixing bowl, stirring well. Add dates and pecans. Spread in prepared pan. Bake at 350 degrees for 25 to 30 minutes or until brown. Remove from pan to cool.

Break crust into small pieces and place in serving dish. Arrange banana slices and mandarin oranges over pieces. Top with layer of whipped topping. Keep refrigerated until serving. Serves 12.

Apple Dapple Cake

NEWBERRY CAFE, NEWBERRY
Lois and Lanny Pickett

Lois added autumn-inspired spices to this popular apple cake recipe that she found in *Best of the Best from Indiana Cookbook.* "This is sort of a fall season dessert," she says, "but I use it some year round. Everyone loves it."

        3 eggs
    1½ cups salad oil
        2 cups sugar
        3 cups flour
        1 teaspoon salt
        1 teaspoon baking soda
        2 teaspoons vanilla extract
        2 teaspoons cinnamon
        1 teaspoon nutmeg
        3 cups peeled, chopped apples (about 4 medium)
    1½ cups chopped pecans
        1 cup brown sugar
      ¼ cup milk
      ½ cup margarine

In a large bowl, mix eggs, oil, and sugar; blend well. Add flour, salt, soda, vanilla, cinnamon, and nutmeg; mix well. Stir in apples and pecans. Pour into well-greased tube or Bundt pan. Bake at 350 degrees for about 1 hour; remove from oven.

For topping, combine brown sugar, milk, and margarine in a small saucepan over medium heat. Bring to a simmer and cook, stirring, for 2½ minutes, making sure sugar is completely dissolved.

Pour topping over cake while cake is still hot. Allow cake to cool; remove from pan when completely cold. Serves 12.

Pineapple Cake

NEWBERRY CAFE, NEWBERRY
Lois and Lanny Pickett

A customer gave Lois the recipe for this moist cake, which she serves topped with a rich, sweet cream cheese frosting. "I use this about once a month," she says. "Even the guys like it."

> 2 **cups flour**
> 2 **cups granulated sugar**
> 2 **teaspoons baking soda**
> 2 **eggs**
> 1 **(20-ounce) can crushed pineapple, with juice**
> 1 **cup chopped pecans**
> ½ **cup butter, softened**
> 1 **(8-ounce) package cream cheese, softened**
> 2 **cups powdered sugar**

In a mixing bowl, stir together flour, granulated sugar, and baking soda. Add eggs and pineapple; mix well. Stir in pecans. Pour into greased 9-by-13-inch pan. Bake at 350 degrees about 35 minutes or until toothpick inserted in center comes out clean. Cool.

For frosting, beat together butter and cream cheese; slowly add powdered sugar and mix well. Spread on cooled cake. Serves 15.

Chocolate Chip Zucchini Nut Cake

MARTY'S BLUEBIRD CAFE, LAKETON
Martha "Marty" and Bart Huffman

This tried and true fudgy cake is a delicious way to utilize zucchini, grown in abundance in backyard gardens across the state. "This is a very moist, rich cake," says Marty, "great warm with a dab of ice cream."

2½ cups flour
1¾ cup sugar
¼ cup cocoa
1 teaspoon baking soda
½ teaspoon salt
½ teaspoon cinnamon
½ cup butter, softened
2 eggs
½ cup buttermilk
1 teaspoon vanilla extract
2 cups grated zucchini
1 cup chocolate chips
crushed walnuts (optional)

Heat oven to 325 degrees. In a large mixing bowl, stir together flour, sugar, cocoa, baking soda, salt, and cinnamon. Add butter, eggs, buttermilk, and vanilla and mix well. Stir in zucchini, chocolate chips, and walnuts, if desired.

Pour batter into greased and floured 9-by-13-inch baking pan. Bake for about 1 hour or until toothpick inserted in middle of cake comes out clean. Serves 15.

Pig Pickin' Cake

BABY BOOMERS CAFE, HAMILTON
Penny Hawkins

This easy recipe, which Penny got from a friend, starts with a packaged cake mix. The end result is a moist, fruity concoction with a fluffy, sweet topping.

> 1 box yellow cake mix
> 4 eggs
> ½ cup vegetable oil
> 1 (11-ounce) can mandarin oranges, with liquid
> 1 (4-ounce) package instant vanilla pudding
> 1 (15-ounce) can crushed pineapple, with juice
> 1 (8-ounce) tub frozen nondairy whipped topping,
>   thawed

Preheat oven to 350 degrees. In a mixing bowl combine cake mix, eggs, oil, and oranges. Pour into lightly greased 9-by-13-inch baking pan. Bake until cake is light brown and toothpick inserted in the middle comes out clean, about 45 minutes.

For icing, combine pudding mix and pineapple; fold in whipped topping. Spread on cooled cake. Serves 12.

Further Reading

Adams, Marcia. *Heartland: The Best of the Old and the New from Midwest Kitchens*. New York: Clarkson N. Potter, 1991.

Bukoff, Allen. "Stalking the Wild Breaded Pork Tenderloin in Iowa." http://www.des-loines.blogspot.com (accessed August 10, 2010).

Dutro, Kathleen M. "Tender(loin) Hearted." *Hoosier Farmer*, Summer 2007, 14–21.

Garrett, Rick. "All Tenderloins, All the Time." http://breadedtenderloin.wordpress.com (accessed August 10, 2010).

Indiana Foodways Alliance. http://indianafoodways.com (accessed August 10, 2010).

Lumbra, Elaine, ed. *The Hoosier Cookbook*. Bloomington: Indiana University Press, 1976.

———. *More Hoosier Cooking*. Bloomington: Indiana University Press, 1982.

McKee, Gwen, and Barbara Moseley, eds. *Best of the Best from Indiana Cookbook*. Brandon, MS: Quail Ridge Press, 1995.

Rombauer, Irma S., Marion Rombauer Becker, and Ethan Becker. *The All New, All Purpose Joy of Cooking*. New York: Scribner's, 1997.

Sohn, Mark F. *Appalachian Home Cooking*. Lexington: University of Kentucky Press, 2005.

Southern Foodways Alliance. http://southernfoodways.com (accessed August 10, 2010).

Stern, Jane, and Michael Stern. *500 Things to Eat Before It's Too Late*. Boston: Houghton Mifflin Harcourt, 2009. The breaded pork tenderloin and pie at Nick's Kitchen in Huntington are featured on pages 290–91.

———. "Love Me Tenderloin." *Gourmet*, January 2003, 22–23.

———. *Roadfood*. New York: Broadway Books, 2008.

Stovall, David. http://porktenderloinsandwich.com (accessed August 10, 2010).

Stradley, Linda. *I'll Have What They're Having: Legendary Local Cuisine*. Guilford, CT: Three Forks, 2002. Indiana sugar cream pie is featured on page 185 and persimmon pudding on page 201. But, gasp! The breaded pork tenderloin has been overlooked.

Stuttgen, Joanne Raetz. *Cafe Indiana*. Madison: University of Wisconsin Press, 2007.

Willard, Pat. *America Eats!* New York: Bloomsbury, 2008. The Bon Ton Cafe in Bainbridge appears on page 59.

Index